THE ULTIMATE

OUTDOOR
COOKBOOK

ALL-DAY MEALS AND DRINKS FOR BACKYARD
ENTERTAINING AND ELEVATED CAMPING FARE

Linda Ly | **Photography by Will Taylor**

HARVARD
COMMON
PRESS

© 2021 Quarto Publishing Group USA Inc.
Text © 2017, 2019 Lynda Ly
Photography © 2017, 2019 Will Taylor

First Published in 2021 by The Harvard Common Press, an imprint of The Quarto Group,
100 Cummings Center, Suite 265-D, Beverly, MA 01915, USA.
T (978) 282-9590 F (978) 283-2742 QuartoKnows.com

The Harvard Common Press titles are also available at discount for retail, wholesale, promotional, and bulk purchase. For details, contact the Special Sales Manager by email at specialsales@quarto.com or by mail at The Quarto Group, Attn: Special Sales Manager, 100 Cummings Center, Suite 265-D, Beverly, MA 01915, USA.

25 24 23 22 21   1 2 3 4 5

ISBN: 978-0-7603-7285-2

The content in this book appeared in the previously published titles *The New Camp Cookbook* (Voyageur Press, 2017) and *The Backyard Fire Cookbook* (The Harvard Common Press, 2019).

Library of Congress Cataloging-in-Publication Data available

Photography: Will Taylor
Illustration: Shutterstock.com

Printed in China

CONTENTS

INTRODUCTION

When I close my eyes and think of my happy place, I picture this: a canopy of conifers with a breeze whipping through, a bubbling creek, or perhaps a glassy lake, with a sublime string of peaks in the distance. Tents and coolers. Logs and embers. A hot, hearty meal shared around the fire with family and friends as the last light fades.

It's no secret I love a good campfire, but, above all, I love a great meal cooked over one. I love the leap and snap of a lively fire as it collapses into red-hot coals. I love the alchemy of sun and smoke that makes those long summer days seem even slower. I love the fact that every time you grill and gather around a fire, it's a community event. You pull up your chairs, clink some cold libations, and sink into conversations that get longer and deeper as the night goes on.

It doesn't matter how simple or elaborate the meal is, or whether I charred it just a tad too much. Food just tastes better outside, and even more so when you're cooking over the one fuel that infuses its own sultry flavor: firewood.

But, as much as I love camping, I can't always get away. I can, however, get outside, even if it's just a few steps from the house. So when I started thinking about how I would follow up the success of *The New Camp Cookbook*, it made sense to bring that kind of cooking closer to home and right into our own backyards—or front yards, or courtyards, or wherever we can carve out space for a fire.

When it comes to grilling, I'm all about live fire. There's a visceral appeal to cooking over wood— think hissing steaks on a bed of smoldering, glowing red coals—that a gas stove and even a gas grill can't match. It's a rugged thrill that's been embedded in our culinary DNA since our human forebears discovered how to put food to flame. If you've ever had the primal exhilaration—not to mention the gustatory pleasure— of roasting a marshmallow or hot dog over an open flame, then you know.

With a live fire, you're not just turning a knob to medium-high and waiting patiently for your food to brown. You're not merely cooking—you're conducting: feeding the flames, moving the coals, or fine-tuning the vents, guiding the grill to a perfect harmony of char and smoke.

The dynamic element of grilling forces you to embrace the experience. It's food that has a beginning, a middle, and an end. You have to slow down, engage your senses, and sometimes improvise the way you cook. At the same time, you expect—even welcome— the imperfections because it's those extra bits of burnt-on crust and deeply caramelized flavors that add complexity and depth. The volatile nature of cooking over fire means your food will never come out exactly like the last time, and that makes it all the more intriguing.

What you *can* be sure of, however, is the way grilling elevates ordinary meals into feasts that feel far more special. Grilling intensifies the natural sweetness of fruits and vegetables and turns meat into a magical blend of molten fat and juicy protein. It seasons food with the flavor of the outdoors, even if you happen to be grilling in the middle of the city.

In this book, you're not going to find low and slow

barbecue or overnight brines, or whole animals tied to iron crosses or spinning on a spit. These are recipes you can make on those low-key nights when you just want to sit in the backyard with a drink in hand, enjoying the colors of a softening sky and the smells of good food sizzling on the grill.

Outside of a campsite, *that* is my happy place—and I hope it's yours as well.

Today's camping menus are no longer confined to the standard fare of franks and beans or "just add water" meals in a bag. They're fresher and healthier, if not a more simplified version of how and what you eat at home.

In this book you'll learn how easy it is for pancakes to come from your own pantry ingredients instead of from boxes. You'll see classic dishes like ratatouille take an interesting turn on the grill as colorful kebabs. Vietnamese bánh mì marries a classic taco in a savory culinary mashup. Shrimp and scallops simmer in a foil pouch of spices, sausages, potatoes, and corn to bring your favorite seafood boil into the woods without the big pot—or the big mess.

While some might be nostalgic, these are not the same recipes you remember from your Scout days, or from family road trips you took every summer as a child. They're inspired by real food and global flavors, and reflect advances in camp cuisine as well as a modern, healthful approach to cooking and eating outdoors. At the same time, they're still fun and unfussy. If your last memory of campfire cooking was

a burnt hot dog on a cold bun, they may even rekindle your love of the live fire.

Away from home and under the open sky, cooking is stripped down to the bare essentials, so food becomes its own adventure—but don't mistake adventure to mean nerve-wracking or hard. Cooking in camp can be as easy or extravagant as you want it to be, but the experience in itself triggers all the senses, making you feel alive and free. There's a definite pleasure in escaping from our reliance on our kitchens, with their sleek appliances and specialized gadgets, and delving deep into our instincts—taming the flames and guiding the elements of nature to a delicious end.

Every time you make a meal or even a single recipe, it may very well turn out a little different than the last time. It could be the brand of charcoal or type of firewood you use, the salty air near the sea, the elevation of your campsite, or the fresh green scent of conifers blowing through the forest. And that's what keeps it so exciting.

Whether you're out for the day or gone on a weeklong road trip, whether you're traveling in a tricked-out trailer with a fully stocked kitchen or sleeping in a whisper-light tent with fire and foil as your primary mode of dinner, this book aims to equip you with the right tools and a repertoire of adaptable recipes for planning, packing, cooking, and eating well in the great outdoors.

CHAPTER 1

GETTING STARTED AND SETTING UP YOUR OUTDOOR KITCHEN

You roll up to the campsite, throw the doors open, and tilt your head back to take in the fresh smell of pine. Your phone shows zero bars of reception. The distractions of home feel worlds away. As the dust settles from your arrival, bins and bags get dragged out of the car. A string of lights goes up in the trees. You pull a cold drink from the cooler, toss another to your sidekick, and start to settle in.

BUILD THE ULTIMATE COOKING FIRE

No matter where we are—out in the woods or in our own backyard—a crackling wood-burning fire can spike all our senses, from sight to smell. No other cooking method compares.

While I love my charcoal grill for the speed and convenience it offers, I leap at the chance to cook over a wood fire if the timing is right and an eager crowd is pulling up their chairs (because what fun is fire without family and friends to share it with?).

Building a fire is also much easier than survival shows make it seem. As long as you have something to start the fire with and a stack of clean seasoned wood, you can get a nice fire going in less time than it takes to finish a tasty cold beverage.

THE THREE STAGES OF BUILDING A WOOD-BURNING FIRE

1. **Tinder:** In a backyard setting, this is usually crumpled paper or a fire starter. You can even get creative with other super combustible materials, such as dryer lint or paper egg cartons.

2. **Kindling:** Once the tinder catches fire, it needs kindling to keep the flames going. A pile of small sticks, twigs, and branches burns just long enough to light the next stage of your fire.

3. **Logs:** The kindling lights the logs on top as it starts to burn down. With proper airflow around the logs and a steady supply of firewood, a fire can be maintained from the first course all the way through dessert and beyond.

Step 1

Step 2

Step 3

How to Make an Old-School Campfire

To allow plenty of time for the fire to burn down into a bed of hot, glowing coals, start your fire at least 45 minutes to 1 hour before you plan to grill. It's easy to keep the fire going once you have it, but not so easy to rush the process of making usable coals.

Step 1: Loosely pile a couple large handfuls of tinder in the center of your fire pit. Make a small teepee around the tinder with the kindling, leaning the sticks against each other for support.

Step 2: Make a second teepee around the first teepee with your smaller logs. Remember to leave a little gap at the bottom so you can reach in easily with a lighter.

Step 3: Light the tinder. As the wood starts burning, continue to add more logs, leaving space for airflow and gradually increasing the size of the logs until the fire is firmly established.

Step 4: Once the logs burn down into ashy red embers, gently break them apart with a grill rake. Rake a large mound of coals toward the front of the fire pit to cook with and keep a small fire going in the back to replenish the coals as needed.

GRILL HACK

To turn your charcoal grill into a wood-burning grill, fill a chimney with chunks of smoking wood and light them, just as you would light charcoal. As the wood burns down into embers, add more wood to top up the chimney. Dump the glowing embers into your grill and start grilling!

How to Light a Chimney

With a chimney starter, you can light a full load of charcoal at once with very little effort.

HOT TIP

When handling lump charcoal, slip a plastic bag over your hand to keep your fingers clean.

Step 1: Remove the top (cooking) grate from your charcoal grill and open all the dampers. (You only need the bottom charcoal grate at this point.) Fill the chimney to the top with charcoal.

Step 2: From here, you have two options to get those coals lit:

    1. *The traditional way:* Stuff a couple sheets of loosely crumpled newspaper in the bottom compartment of the chimney, then set it on the charcoal grate. Tilt the chimney slightly to encourage airflow and light the paper with a lighter. Stand the chimney upright and wait for the coals to catch.

    2. *With a fire starter:* Place it on the charcoal grate and light it. Set the chimney directly on top of the fire starter and let the flames do their thing.

Step 3: About 15 to 20 minutes after you light the chimney, flames will dance out the top and the charcoal will start to turn gray with ash. At this stage, the coals should be sufficiently lit to pour into the grill.

GRILL HACK

No chimney starter? No problem. Open the bottom vent on your grill all the way and place eight to ten sheets of crumpled newspaper (or two or three fire starters) below the bottom grate. Pile the charcoal evenly across the bottom grate and light the paper or fire starters. Once the charcoal is coated in ash, set the top grate in place. (Keep in mind that using paper with this method leaves behind more ash.)

Creating Cooking Zones

Once your coals are ashed over and piled on the bottom of your fire pit or grill, you have to decide how you'll be cooking: direct or indirect heat?

Direct heat is hot and fast. You place the food on the grate directly over the coals for a blast of heat that gives it those beautiful grill marks, a burnished crust, and crispy skin. Direct heat is ideal for searing meats and browning vegetables, and for grilling quick-cooking foods such as seafood, bread, and cheese.

Indirect heat is moderate and slow. The food is placed on the grate over a heat-free zone and cooked by the heat of the coals banked on the side. This allows slower-cooking foods (such as whole chickens and hefty cuts of pork and beef) more time to cook through on the inside without burning on the outside.

There are numerous ways to arrange a fire, depending on what you're cooking and how much heat you need.

SINGLE-LEVEL FIRE

Spread an even layer of coals, one or two coals deep, across the bottom of a fire pit or grill. This creates a medium-hot fire that's the sweet spot for direct grilling most foods. Adjust the thickness of the layer to reduce or increase the heat as needed.

TWO-ZONE FIRE

Bank all the coals to one side of the fire pit or grill, leaving the other side empty for a completely cool zone. This versatile arrangement allows for direct and indirect grilling, as well as a coal-free zone if your food is charring too quickly or causing flare-ups. Aim to leave at least one-third of the grill empty as a safety zone or warming rack.

Single-Level Fire

Two-Zone Fire

Three-Zone Fire

THREE-ZONE FIRE

Bank the coals to each side of the grill and leave the middle empty. This creates an indirect cooking zone in the center of the grill with heat coming from both sides, allowing your food to cook evenly without the need to rotate halfway through.

HOT TIP

Movies like to seduce us with images of food cooking over a roaring fire. But unless you're roasting marshmallows, flames that leap and lick at your food are not optimal for grilling, as they often result in an over-charred exterior and an undercooked interior. While small flames are fine, you don't want your food engulfed in fire, no matter how awesome it looks. Wait until the wood burns down into glowing red coals, which gives you more control over the heat.

How Hot Are the Coals?

Many charcoal grills come with thermometers built into the lid, which are capable of giving you the approximate temperature at the level of the thermometer probe—sometimes more than 6 inches (15 cm) above the cooking grate. While this can be useful for indirect grilling, it's not truly indicative of what the actual temperature is at the cooking grate itself.

For direct grilling, the easiest way to gauge the temperature of your grilling surface is with your hand—no matter how high the grate sits above the coals. Though this may sound even less precise than relying on a thermometer, much of grilling is based on your senses, and holding your hand above the grate will give you a better sense of heat.

THE HAND CHECK

Hover your hand about 3 inches (7.5 cm) above the cooking grate. Count the number of seconds you can hold your hand there comfortably before you have to

TIME	HEAT LEVEL	GRILL TEMPERATURE
1 to 2 seconds	Hot	450°F to 550°F (230°C to 290°C)
2 to 4 seconds	Medium-hot	400°F to 425°F (200°C to 220°C)
4 to 5 seconds	Medium	350°F to 375°F (180°C to 190°C)
More than 5 seconds	Medium-low to low	Ideal for warming (these lower temperatures are also where smoking, or true barbecue, comes in)

pull back. Temperature fluctuations and hot spots are inevitable, so check a few spots before you start grilling.

Refueling Your Cooking Fire

If your recipe calls for a cooking time of more than 30 minutes, it's a good idea to have more coals ready so you can maintain steady heat.

For a wood fire, simply keep a small fire going in the back of the fire pit and periodically feed it with more logs to produce more coals. Rake the coals over to your cooking area as needed.

For a charcoal fire, scatter a few chunks of unlit hardwood lump charcoal on top of the embers. Leave the grill lid open for a few minutes until the fresh charcoal catches fire.

How to Dispose of Wood Ash

With a **charcoal grill**, good grilling habits include emptying the ash catcher before (or after) each use. I like to empty mine before I start grilling, as the ashes from the previous session will have cooled for at least 24 hours. Carefully remove the ash catcher (as there may still be hot embers lingering in the ash) and dump the contents into an ash bucket with a tight-fitting lid. Let the ashes cool completely for several days, after which they can be used in the garden, disposed of in a green waste bin, or placed in the trash.

With a **fire pit**, let the ashes cool for at least 24 hours so they're safer to handle. Collect the ashes into an ash bucket to cool for several days, then use them in the garden or place them in a green waste bin or trash can.

Unlike charcoal briquettes, which are full of additives, hardwood and hardwood lump charcoal are natural products that burn down into nutrient-rich ashes. The wood ash can be used as fertilizer in a garden or added to a compost pile. Because it's highly alkaline, use sparingly if you're not certain of your soil pH. Throw out any extra ash.

START GRILLING

Now that you know how to build a fire in a fire pit (see page 10), how to light a chimney (see page 12), how to create cooking zones (see page 13), and how to gauge the temperature of your grilling surface (see page 16), it's time to put it all together!

Step 1: Fire it up: If you're going to cook over a wood fire, give it at least 45 minutes to 1 hour to burn down into glowing embers. If you're going to cook over charcoal, light the chimney at least 20 minutes before you want to start grilling.

Step 2: Arrange the coals: Once all the coals are lightly covered in gray ash, use a grill rake to arrange them into a single-level, two-zone, or three-zone fire. Set the cooking grate in place, if using, and let it preheat for about 10 minutes. If you're working with a charcoal

grill, adjust the vents as needed to reach your desired temperature. (Learn more about venting on page 159.)

Step 3: Clean and oil the grate: There are several ways to clean a grate, with my favorite being a Grate Chef Grill Wipe for its effectiveness and convenience. If you've neglected to clean the grate after your last grilling session, start with a good scrub using a grill brush when the grate is hot (as the heat helps release any food remnants). Follow up with several passes of the grill wipe, using one side to clean the grate *before* you start grilling, saving the other side to clean the grate *after* you finish grilling. Aside from oiling the grate, the wipe picks up any greasy residue left behind by the brush, as well as possible stray brush bristles.

As an alternative to a grill wipe, you can do it the old-fashioned way: wad up a paper towel (or some aluminum foil), hold it with tongs, mist the towel with high-heat cooking spray, and wipe down the hot grate.

Another fun method for cleaning and oiling a grate is to use an onion. Cut a small onion in half, spear it with a barbecue fork, and mist the cut side with high-heat cooking spray. Rub the onion firmly over the hot grate. The juices and oil work to loosen any burnt-on bits, wipe away grime, and lubricate the grate.

WARNING

Avoid spraying oil directly onto a grate as it's heating up.

If you're grilling corn, shuck the ears and save the green husks. Wad up the husks, grip the wad with tongs, and mist with high-heat cooking spray. Watch your friends marvel at your ingenuity as you clean and oil the grill with it!

Step 4: Finally, food! When it's time to place the food on the grate, here are a few of my favorite tips for grilling more efficiently:

+ **Arrange the food in a logical fashion.** Place pieces from left to right (or back to front) so you know what went on first and what might need to be turned first or come off the grill first.

+ **Don't overcrowd the grate.** Leave at least 1 to 2 inches (2.5 to 5 cm) of space between pieces of food so the sides cook evenly and you have room to work.

+ **Grill on the diagonal.** If you want professional-looking grill marks on your steaks, chops, or other flat, wide foods, place them diagonal to the bars on the grate. After a couple of minutes, rotate the food a quarter turn to make a handsome crosshatch of grill marks.

+ **Make the most of your fire by using it to the very end.** Throw on a few vegetables to round out your meal or grill other food to save for lunch the next day. If your fire has gotten very low, remove the grate and put some onions, garlic, or elephant garlic directly on the embers to roast while you eat. (See page 65 for a list of other foods that cook well in the coals.) These flavorful ingredients can be used for making salads, sandwiches, scrambles, and noodle and rice bowls throughout the week.

Step 5: Clean and oil the grate again: The last thing you probably want to do after you cook is clean, but a quick swipe of a grill brush (while the grate is still hot) can save you a lot of elbow grease in the end. Just run the brush over the grate a few times to dislodge any debris and continue with your meal. You can return to the grill at the end of the day (or even the next morning) to polish it off with a grill wipe.

KNOW WHEN YOUR FOOD IS DONE

Grilling is an art that relies on all your senses to properly judge when your food is done. With heat being variable across different fire pits and grills, not to mention the type of wood or charcoal used, and even how the weather is that day, you can't always trust the timing in any particular recipe. But, you can train and trust your senses.

See. A lot of what you need to know is in plain sight: the blackened kernels on an ear of corn, the deep brown crust on a scallop, the glistening char on chicken skin, or the tone of red inside that shows you how well the steak is done.

Hear. That oh-so-satisfying hiss of a burger landing on the grill, or the steady hum of a stew bubbling in a Dutch oven, are good indicators that tell you how high or low the heat is.

Smell. Properly grilled food has an intoxicating aroma deeply rooted in our ancestral history: warm, earthy, smoky, caramelized, sometimes evoking hints of sage or grass. You will always stop and notice the smell of good barbecue wafting through the air. It's programmed in all of us.

Touch. How something feels is important, too: the tenderness of charred vegetables, the crispness of pizza crust, or the gentle give of bread pudding and pancakes.

Taste. And, of course, that first bite will always let you know whether your food needs more or (needed!) less time on the grill.

Grilling Temperatures for Meats

Beyond your senses, the only accurate way to measure the doneness of meats is to use an instant-read thermometer. The United States Department of Agriculture (USDA) and other national food safety agencies have official recommendations for "safe" cooking temperatures, but my preferences are sometimes lower or higher than their guidelines. If you choose to go lower for some meats (steak is a good example), you need to balance your desire for more favorable textures with safety. On the other hand, while dark meat chicken is safe to eat at 165°F (74°C), I find it is at its juiciest and most tender at higher temperatures, when the heat has had time to break down tough connective tissue.

BEEF	TEMPERATURE
Rare	115°F to 120°F; 120°F to 125°F after resting (46°C to 49°C; 49°C to 52°C after resting)
Medium-rare	120°F to 125°F; 125°F to 130°F after resting (49°C to 52°C; 52°C to 54°C after resting)
Medium	130°F to 135°F; 135°F to 140°F after resting (54°C to 57°C; 57°C to 60°C after resting)
Medium-well	140°F to 145°F; 145°F to 150°F after resting (60°C to 63°C; 63°C to 65.5°C after resting)
Well-done	150°F to 155°F; 155°F to 160°F after resting (65.5°C to 68°C; 68°C to 71°C after resting)

PORK	TEMPERATURE
Medium	140°F to 145°F; 150°F after resting (60°C to 63°C; 65.5°C after resting)
Well-done	150°F to 155°F; 160°F after resting (65.5°C to 68°C; 71°C after resting)

CHICKEN	TEMPERATURE
White meat	165°F (74°C)
Dark meat	180°F to 185°F (82°C to 85°C)

Carryover Cooking

On a grill, the exterior of the meat heats much more quickly than the interior, resulting in a large difference in temperature between the surface and the center of the meat. This is why temperatures are always taken in the center—and thickest—part of the flesh.

When you take the meat off the grill, heat on the meat's surface continues to travel inward, causing the internal temperature of the meat to rise. This phenomenon of food continuing to cook after it's removed from the heat source is called carryover cooking. It's also an important reason you should take meats off the grill *before* they reach your target temperature for doneness, as they continue to rise 5 to 10 degrees while resting.

Meats with more thermal mass, such as roasts and thick cuts of steak, absorb more heat during grilling and have a greater amount of carryover. Thin cuts, like skirt steaks, don't have time to build up a large heat reservoir so there is very little carryover. While carryover cooking can also occur in poultry, it's best to cook chicken to proper doneness for safety reasons.

The Importance of Resting

Resting meat is an essential part of grilling. When meat is left to sit after being taken off the grill, the muscle fibers relax and allow the internal juices to redistribute throughout the roast or cut. This results in juicier, more flavorful meat.

As a general rule, the thicker the meat, the more resting time it needs. Steaks benefit from 5 to 10 minutes of rest while large roasts need at least 15 minutes. Combined with carryover cooking, resting helps ensure your food is cooked perfectly to your taste.

I usually let steaks rest as I plate them for my guests. By the time the table is set, drinks are refilled, and everyone digs in, it's just the right amount of time for the meat to come up to temperature.

FIRE SAFETY

Grilling often involves a crowd of people and some alcohol, so it's not uncommon to let things slide when you're having a good time. To make sure the fire stays *inside* the grill, keep these safety points in mind.

+ Don't grill under eaves or overhangs, patio covers, tree branches, or other combustible objects.

+ Pay attention when grilling on a wooden deck or in an area with a lot of dry grass and bushes. If needed, hose down those areas with water before you start grilling.

+ Pay extra attention in windy weather, as sparks can fly off the grill.

+ If you have a fire pit, it's a good idea to keep a bucket of sand nearby for smothering grease fires.

+ With open fire pits, have a reliable water source handy in case you need to douse floating embers.

+ Keep a large box of salt or baking soda on hand for smothering small grease fires in a grill. A little refrigerator-size carton is not going to cut it.

+ And, most importantly, get a Class K, B, or ABC fire extinguisher and know how to use it. Service it annually and check the pressure gauge periodically to ensure it's in working order.

Preventing Flare-Ups

Flare-ups happen when fats drip off the meat and into the hot coals. You can control flare-ups by trimming excess fat from meats, patting excess oil from marinated meats with a paper towel, or using a two-zone fire for cooking. If a flare-up occurs, simply move the meat to the cool (empty) side of the grill until the fire dies down, then move it back over direct heat to finish cooking. Closing the grill lid will also control minor flare-ups by snuffing out the flames.

I don't recommend using a spray bottle of water to shoot down flare-ups, as this will usually lead to an ash film on your food.

What to Do If Your Grill Catches Fire

While flare-ups are a normal part of the grilling process, more serious fires can pose a danger to you and your grill. Sometimes, the grease that accumulates at the bottom of your grill (in a drip pan, for instance) or on a plancha can catch fire. Act fast! Close the grill lid to contain the flames. Slide the dampers shut to starve the fire of oxygen and wait for it to burn out.

For small grease fires, you can also try smothering them with salt or baking soda. It takes a lot of salt or baking soda to do this, so keep a full box stashed in your outdoor kitchen. (Note that other baking products, like baking powder or flour, will *not* help and will only make the fire worse.)

WARNING

Never use water to put out a grease fire. Pouring water on the flames can cause the oil to splash and spread the fire farther.

COOKING ON A CAMP STOVE

A camp stove is a necessity when camping. Whether it's boiling water for your morning coffee or stir-frying vegetables for a family dinner, a good camp stove lets you cook anything in camp that you typically cook at home. It's the fastest and simplest way to start any meal, because you don't have to light a chimney or build a fire. Just turn on the stove, dial up the heat, and you're good to go.

While camp stoves offer a narrow window of adjustability from low to high heat, wind and cold weather outside can greatly affect the output of the flame. A more accurate way to measure heat on a cooking surface—in the absence of a cooking thermometer—is with your hand. (See **The Hand Check** on page 16.)

Every recipe in this book gives a range of cooking times and temperatures, but due to variability in camp stoves, cookware, and outdoor conditions, it's ultimately best to rely on sensory cues (how the food looks, smells, and tastes) to determine when your food is fully cooked.

TIPS FOR COOKING AT HIGH ALTITUDES

Cooking in the mountains can come with challenges, even when you aren't baking. The low pressure at high altitude leads to lower boiling points and less heat output—meaning water will boil at a lower temperature and foods will take longer to cook. (This is why, for example, boiling water in Denver is never as hot as boiling water in Los Angeles.)

Since recipes are designed to cook at sea level, it can be difficult to figure out how to account for elevation when the present atmospheric conditions also play a part in how your food cooks. With that in mind, here are a few tips for tweaking recipes when you're camping above 3,000 feet (900 m).

+ Pasta and rice take a little longer to cook at higher elevations. Add 15 to 20 percent more liquid and increase the cooking time by 1 minute for every 1,000 feet (300 m) of elevation.

+ The broth in soups and stews evaporates quicker during cooking, so add 25 percent more liquid than called for in the recipe and increase the cooking time by 2 minutes for every 1,000 feet (300 m) of elevation.

+ Because of lower humidity, watch for meats that might dry out on the grill. Move them to indirect heat (or brush on more sauce) to maintain moisture as needed.

+ Baked goods are prone to being dry and crumbly, and as a result they go stale more quickly. Slightly increase the amount of liquid or egg in the recipe by 1 to 2 tablespoons at 3,000 feet (900 m), and add 1½ teaspoons for each additional 1,000 feet (300 m). Sometimes, simply using extra-large eggs can do the trick.

FOOD AND FOREST SAFETY

Being outside, basking in the sun, cooking in camp . . . all of it can make us feel giddy and carefree as much as it can make us care*less* with everyday risks we often don't think about at home. As with any outdoor situation, you can never be too prepared or cautious, especially if you're camping with a large group where small details may be overlooked. Brushing up on a few basics for handling food properly and keeping a clean campsite will make the experience more enjoyable for not only you and your group, but also other campers.

Handling and Preparing Food Safely

Since sanitation is limited in camp, it's important to maintain a scrupulously clean kitchen. No one wants to bring home food poisoning as a souvenir! Just because you're outside and being liberal with the "5-second rule" doesn't mean you can slack on your food safety routine. The safety precautions you take when cooking at home don't change when you're cooking in camp—they become even more important.

When it comes to food safety, these five key points should always be in the front of your mind:

+ Keep your cooler at 40°F (4°C) or below at all times. (Bring a fridge thermometer for peace of mind.)

+ Never leave food out for a prolonged period of time. If food is sitting in the "danger zone" between 40°F and 140°F (4°C and 60°C), it needs to be used within 2 hours (and discarded after that). Keep it in the cooler, warm it on the stove, or use other methods to keep cold foods cold and hot foods hot within that time frame.

+ Cook all meats to proper internal temperatures.

+ Avoid cross-contamination between raw meats and other foods.

+ Always wash your hands before and after handling food.

Frequent hand washing is your best defense against foodborne illnesses. Always keep alcohol-based hand sanitizers accessible in the kitchen as well as in your tent and pack, or better yet, wash your hands (including under your fingernails) with soap and water. To simplify cleanup, heat a pot of water on the stove while you're prepping or eating so you'll have hot water handy when it's time to wash.

Camp kitchens often necessitate the need to reuse dishes and utensils when preparing meals, and while this is a smart method for streamlining your camp flow, it can spell trouble if surfaces are contaminated. Remember to wash all items that come in contact with raw meats, as well as allergens like peanuts if you're cooking for food-sensitive campmates.

Working with raw meats and seafood, in particular, require additional attention in camp. Without the luxury of a refrigerator and running water, the challenges of safely handling them are multiplied.

+ Use a separate meat cooler if possible, or place raw meats in the bottom of a cooler to prevent their juices from dripping onto other food.

+ Securely bag or double-bag all raw meats, or store them in watertight containers.

+ Keep raw meats away from other food and use separate cutting boards and utensils when working with them.

+ Discard used marinades immediately, or boil them for 10 minutes before using as a baste or glaze for your meats.

WARNING

Keep It Clean. If you have to handle a lot of raw meats or seafood in camp, bring a pair of disposable gloves—it'll keep your hands odor-free and mess-free, and allow you to work more efficiently when water sources may be scarce.

Safe Storage Times for Chilled Foods

The following table lists safe storage times for perishables stored in a cooler at 40°F (4°C) or below.

Raw ground meat and ground poultry	1 to 2 days
Raw beef, veal, pork, and lamb	3 to 5 days
Raw chicken and turkey	1 to 2 days
Bacon	2 weeks (unopened package) 1 week (opened package)
Raw sausage (from meat or poultry)	1 to 2 days
Hard sausage (such as pepperoni or jerky)	3 weeks (opened package)
Hot dogs	2 weeks (unopened package) 1 week (opened package)
Egg, chicken, tuna, ham, and macaroni salads	3 to 5 days
Cooked meat, poultry, and fish	3 to 4 days
Soups and stews	3 to 4 days
Raw fish and shellfish	1 to 2 days
Eggs (raw, in shell)	3 to 5 weeks
Eggs (raw, out of shell)	2 to 4 days
Eggs (hard-boiled)	1 week
Liquid pasteurized eggs and egg substitutes	10 days (unopened) 3 days (opened)
Cooked egg dishes	3 to 4 days
Milk	1 week
Butter	2 weeks
Buttermilk, sour cream, and cream cheese	2 weeks

Safe Internal Temperatures for Cooked Meats

A meat thermometer is useful if you're uncertain when your food is fully cooked. Insert it into the thickest part of the flesh to test for the following USDA-recommended internal temperatures.

Beef, pork, lamb, and veal (roasts, steaks, and chops)	145°F (63°C) and allow to rest for at least 3 minutes
Ground beef, pork, lamb, and veal	160°F (71°C)
Hot dogs	165°F (74°C)
Poultry breast meat and dark meat	165°F (74°C)
Ground poultry	165°F (74°C)

Dishwashing in the Wild

Dishwashing isn't the first task I typically leap at the chance to do (compared to the fun of, say, setting up the kitchen and accompanying bar), but give me pretty views, fresh mountain air, and dappled sun on the table, and doing dishes seems less of a chore in camp than it does at home.

A designated dishwashing station at your campsite makes cleanup a breeze, and uses less water and soap than washing in a sink with running water. Pack the following supplies in your gear bin and you'll always be prepared when it's time to clear the table.

Washtubs. You need at least two large tubs for washing and rinsing. If you camp with a large group and do a lot of dishes, a third tub might come in handy. Plastic tubs that nest are perfect for this purpose, but collapsible tubs or sinks can be more convenient storage-wise.

Dish rack or mesh bag. You can certainly spread your dishes out on the table to dry, but a dish rack keeps everything tidier. Look for racks that fold, collapse, or nest neatly inside your washtubs. If you want to travel light, you can toss all your camping dishes in a mesh bag and hang it from a tree to air-dry.

Kitchen towel. Bring at least one towel for drying dishes, drying your hands, or a multitude of other kitchen tasks.

Scrubby sponge or dish brush. And if you cook with cast iron, a plastic scraper is useful for removing residue from your pan without removing the seasoning.

Biodegradable soap. Stick with a highly concentrated, environmentally friendly soap like Dr. Bronner's or Campsuds. A little goes a long way!

If you asked ten people how to clean dishes in camp, you'll get ten different answers. A lot of it depends on the size of your group and the amenities in your campground, but the following method has always worked for me in the widest variety of situations. Here's how it's done:

1. **Scrape.** Scrape any food scraps and uneaten food into a trash bag. Give greasy dishes a wipe with a paper towel. The goal is to get as few food remnants as possible in the washtub.

2. **Soak.** Fill the first washtub with warm water and a few squirts of soap and soak your dishes and utensils. The sooner you do this after a meal, the easier it will be to clean.

3. **Wash.** Squirt a little more soap on your sponge and get to work.

DISHWASHING DON'T

Never wash your dirty dishes at the communal spigots. Doing so leaves an unsightly and unsanitary mess of food scraps in the drain for fellow campers.

4. **Rinse.** Dunk the soapy dishes in the second tub of water to rinse.

5. **Dry.** Let the clean dishes drip dry.

6. **Repeat with pots and pans.** Once all the dishware is done, wash and rinse your cookware using the same method. If your pots and pans have a lot of grease or burnt-on bits, pour a little water in them and boil for a few minutes to soften the residue before you start scrubbing.

7. **Dispose of the dishwater.** Strain the dirty dishwater from the first tub with a fine sieve or mesh screen placed over the second tub. Toss the food particles in the trash. If the campground doesn't have a cleaning facility for gray water disposal, carry the gray water away from camp (at least 200 feet (61 m) from any natural water sources) and fling it far and wide, preferably in a sunny spot so it evaporates quickly. Alternatively, you can dig a hole 6 to 8 inches (15 to 20 cm) deep for dumping all of your gray water so that food smells are contained to one area.

Food Waste Disposal

One of the cardinal rules of camping is to leave the campsite cleaner than you found it. Food waste, in particular, can spoil a beautiful setting as well as mar the overall experience of camping. You've seen it at some point: empty beer bottles in the fire pit, banana peels in the bushes, used napkins buried in leaf litter. Do your part as a responsible steward of our public lands by disposing of trash properly when you're camping.

If you're packing consumables from home, take them out of any unnecessary packaging to reduce bulk and cut down on trash. Repackage food in resealable plastic bags or containers that can be reused for other things. Buy beer in cans to lessen the chances of broken glass as well as lighten your load.

Try to cook only what you know you can eat. Avoiding leftovers—and the dilemma of what to do with them—is essential for maintaining a clean camp, reducing the likelihood of food contamination, and deterring animals from digging through your kitchen.

If you're unable to eat those last few bites off your plate, scrape the food into a trash bag so you don't dirty your wash water (see **Dishwashing in the Wild**, page 25) with excess food remnants.

Place all of your trash in a heavy-duty drawstring bag and hang it from a line or tree. Always keep your trash bag off the ground so it stays out of reach of critters. If the campground doesn't have onsite trash disposal, be sure to pack the trash out with you.

TIPS FOR CAMPING IN BEAR COUNTRY

+ If you're not able to use a bear box or hang your food from a tree, a bear-proof cooler with a padlock can be a wise investment. Stash it at least 100 feet (30.5 m) away (preferably 200 feet (61 m) or more, and downwind) from your campsite when you leave for the day or turn in for the night.

+ Avoid storing food, food containers, or other scented items (such as toothpaste and insect repellent) in your car and especially your tent. Store cosmetics and toiletries with your food when not in use.

+ Never leave food unattended. It takes just a few minutes for not only bears, but also crows, chipmunks, mice, and other pests to raid your kitchen and daypacks when you least expect them.

+ Do not cook next to your tent or leave dirty dishes in camp.

+ Keep the clothes you sleep in free of food and cooking smells.

+ In isolated areas, leaving a bright light on at night can help deter bears from rummaging through your campsite (but is not a substitute for proper storage and cleanup procedures).

+ Food waste should be treated the same as food. If bear-resistant trash cans aren't available in the campground, trash should be stored in a bear box, hung from a tree, or stashed in a secure container and moved at least 100 feet (30.5 m) downwind from camp. Avoid leaving trash bags loose in camp overnight, as you may find yourself waking up to a large mess all over the ground!

+ Camping and cooking in grizzly territory requires extra caution. Always check with local rangers about wildlife activity in the areas you visit.

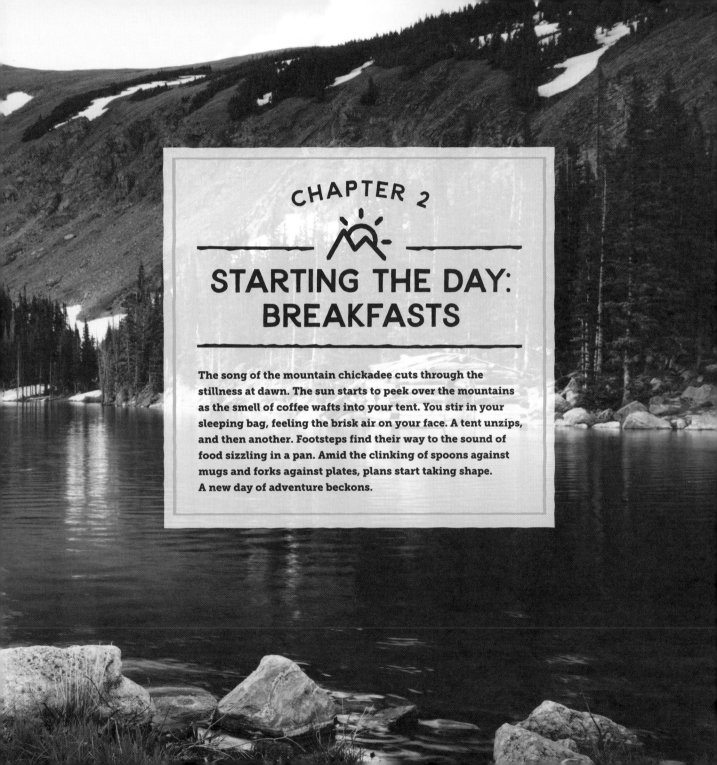

CHAPTER 2

STARTING THE DAY: BREAKFASTS

The song of the mountain chickadee cuts through the stillness at dawn. The sun starts to peek over the mountains as the smell of coffee wafts into your tent. You stir in your sleeping bag, feeling the brisk air on your face. A tent unzips, and then another. Footsteps find their way to the sound of food sizzling in a pan. Amid the clinking of spoons against mugs and forks against plates, plans start taking shape. A new day of adventure beckons.

BLUEBERRY SKILLET SCONES WITH LEMON GLAZE

Fresh, warm, homemade pastries at camp? Yes, please! Skillet scones are a campside take on Irish soda farls, the traditional quick-cooking breads made the old-fashioned way on a griddle. They're crisp and dry on the outside but soft and dense in the center, and are delicious with a smear of jam or butter served alongside coffee or tea. To make a savory version of these skillet scones, just swap the sugar, lemon zest, and blueberries for shredded Cheddar and chopped scallions.

MAKES 14 SCONES

FOR THE SCONES

2 cups (240 g) Multipurpose Baking Mix (page 32)

¾ cup (180 ml) buttermilk

¼ cup (56 g) butter, melted and cooled, plus more for greasing

3 tablespoons granulated sugar

1 large egg

Zest of 1 large lemon

1 cup (170 g) blueberries

FOR THE GLAZE

½ cup (57 g) powdered sugar

1 tablespoon lemon juice

To make the scones, in a large bowl, stir together the baking mix, buttermilk, butter, granulated sugar, egg, and lemon zest with a large sturdy spoon until a soft, sticky, and shaggy dough forms. Gently fold in the blueberries.

Grease a large skillet with butter and heat it over medium-low heat. Using a large spoon, drop ¼-cupfuls of dough (slightly larger than a golf ball) into the skillet. Arrange them so that the sides of each biscuit are barely touching. You should have 14 scones.

Cover and cook until the scones are golden brown on the bottom, 4 to 5 minutes. Turn each biscuit over with a spoon and continue cooking, covered, for about 5 minutes more until both sides are lightly browned and the scones are fully cooked in the center.

Meanwhile, to make the glaze, whisk together the powdered sugar and lemon juice in a small bowl until well blended. Drizzle the glaze over the warm scones before serving.

✧ USE IT UP ✧

Want to find a recipe for that buttermilk left in the carton? Use it up in Buttermilk Pancakes with Maple, Mascarpone, and Berries (page 40) or Dutch Oven–Baked Buttermilk Pancake with Raspberries and Almonds (page 124).

MULTIPURPOSE BAKING MIX

Freshly made baked goods—that don't come out of a box or can—feel like such a luxury in camp, even though their core ingredients couldn't be simpler. But hauling bags of flour, sugar, and leaveners isn't really feasible, nor is all the exact measuring you have to do every time for every recipe. If you bring a large batch of this highly versatile baking mix, however, you can whip up homemade cobblers (page 227), scones (page 30), pancakes (pages 39 and 40), biscuits, coffee cakes, and other quick breads with ease. It also works in other recipes that call for commercial all-purpose baking mixes. Double or triple the recipe according to your needs.

MAKES 3 CUPS (360 G)

3 cups (360 g) all-purpose flour

1 tablespoon sugar

1 tablespoon baking powder

1 teaspoon baking soda

1 teaspoon kosher salt

Combine all of the ingredients in a medium bowl. Transfer to a resealable plastic bag or lidded container and store in a dry, cool place for up to 8 months. Before using, stir the mix around to evenly distribute the ingredients.

RECIPE NOTE
I use the "scoop and sweep" method for measuring flour: simply scoop a heaping cupful of flour, then level it with a straightedge. If your flour has been sitting in the bottom of a bag or canister for a while, fluff it up with a fork before scooping.

CHAI-SPICED OATMEAL WITH CINNAMON APPLES

If you like to start the day with a hot mug of chai, you're sure to love this bowl of chai-spiced oatmeal. A few spoon-fuls of chai concentrate turn ordinary oatmeal into a rich and creamy breakfast that's as cozy and comforting as the tea itself. Apples and walnuts are a classic combination for sweetness and crunch, but you can also try pears, bananas, pepitas, or pecans. If you don't want to dirty another pan, nix the fresh fruit altogether and stir in a handful of raisins and dates.

MAKES 4 SERVINGS

3 cups (700 ml) water

2 cups (225 g) Toasted Instant Oatmeal (page 36)

6 tablespoons Chai Concentrate (page 244)

2 tablespoons butter

2 medium apples, cored and thinly sliced

⅛ teaspoon ground cinnamon

Chopped walnuts

Bring the water to a boil in a small saucepan and add the oats. Reduce the heat and simmer for about 5 minutes, stirring occasionally, until the oats are cooked to your preferred consistency. Stir in the chai concentrate and heat just enough to keep warm.

Meanwhile, melt the butter in a large skillet over medium heat. Add the apples and cinnamon and cook until tender, about 5 minutes, stirring occasionally.

Divide the oatmeal and apples among 4 bowls and top each with a handful of walnuts before serving.

SAVORY OATMEAL WITH SHIITAKE AND SPINACH

In this savory spin on oatmeal, the grains give ricelike texture to a hearty, Asian-inspired breakfast bowl that can hold its own at other times of day. Using chicken broth in place of water amps up the umami factor—and you can try this trick for concocting your own savory oatmeal. If you have leftover cooked chicken from the night before, toss that into the pan too.

MAKES 4 SERVINGS

2 tablespoons olive oil, divided

1 medium shallot, finely chopped

3 cups (700 ml) chicken broth

2 cups (225 g) Toasted Instant Oatmeal (page 36), no added sugar or cinnamon

8 medium shiitake mushrooms, sliced (about 3 ounces)

¼ teaspoon kosher salt

⅛ teaspoon ground black pepper

3 cups (100 g) packed baby spinach

2 tablespoons ponzu sauce, plus more for serving

RECIPE NOTE
Ponzu sauce is a Japanese citrus-based soy sauce found in the ethnic aisle of most well-stocked supermarkets.

Drizzle 1 tablespoon of the oil in a small saucepan over medium-high heat. Add the shallots and cook until they start to turn translucent, about 2 minutes. Add the broth and oatmeal and bring to a boil. Reduce the heat and simmer for about 5 minutes, stirring occasionally, until the oats are cooked to your preferred consistency. Continue to heat just enough to keep warm.

Meanwhile, set a large skillet over medium-high heat and swirl in the remaining 1 tablespoon oil. Add the mushrooms, salt, and pepper. Cook until the mushrooms are soft, 3 to 5 minutes, stirring occasionally. Add the spinach and ponzu, stir to combine, and cook until the spinach is just wilted, about 2 minutes.

Divide the oatmeal, mushrooms, and spinach among 4 bowls and drizzle with a little ponzu before serving.

TOASTED INSTANT OATMEAL

Many people have fond memories of starting their morning in camp by firing up the stove and tearing open a little packet of instant oatmeal. But you can actually make your own instant oatmeal quite easily with less cost and more control over quality and flavor. Start with rolled oats (also called old-fashioned oats), put them through a couple of extra steps, and they suddenly get more interesting. Here, a light toast in the oven imparts a nutty flavor to the oats, while whizzing half of them in a food processor gives the cooked oatmeal a creamier texture than rolled oats alone.

MAKES 4 CUPS (450 G)

4 cups (400 g) rolled oats

¼ cup (50 g) packed brown sugar (optional, see Note)

1 teaspoon kosher salt

½ teaspoon ground cinnamon (optional, see Note)

RECIPE NOTE

If your preference is for savory oatmeal (like Savory Oatmeal with Bacon, Cheddar, and Fried Egg, opposite page) or you like to control the amount of sweetness in each serving, leave out the brown sugar and cinnamon. Conversely, you can also add more sugar if you typically like your oatmeal sweeter.

Preheat the oven to 350°F (180°C or gas mark 4).

Spread the oats on a rimmed baking sheet and bake for 10 to 15 minutes, stirring halfway through, until lightly toasted but not browned. Let cool.

Put half the toasted oats in a food processor and pulse until finely crumbled. Combine all the oats in a large bowl and stir in the sugar, salt, and cinnamon.

Transfer to a resealable plastic bag or lidded container and store in a dry, cool place for up to 1 year. (Alternatively, you can divide the oatmeal into ½-cup [57-g] portions and store them individually to make your own instant oatmeal packets.)

✧ MIX IT UP ✧

If you're making your own instant oatmeal packets, mix in your favorite flavorings ahead of time and all that's needed when you're ready to cook is a pot of boiling water. Try any combination of dried fruits (dates, apricots, cranberries), freeze-dried fruits (strawberries, blueberries, apples), seeds (chia, flax, hemp), and other add-ins (coconut flakes, candied ginger, powdered milk). I like to keep nuts separate, added only when the oatmeal is done so they retain their crunch.

SAVORY OATMEAL WITH BACON, CHEDDAR, AND FRIED EGG

If sweet oatmeal has never been your thing, savory oatmeal may just change your mind about the classic breakfast bowl. Let the traditionalists top their oatmeal with fruits, nuts, and milk; the rebel in you knows that bacon makes everything better. Cheddar adds even more punch to every bite, and an egg—fried in bacon grease, of course—fuels you up for the day's big hike (or big hammock fest, if that's more your speed).

MAKES 4 SERVINGS

1 tablespoon olive oil

1 small yellow onion, finely chopped

3 cups (700 g) water

2 cups (225 g) Toasted Instant Oatmeal (page 36), with no added sugar or cinnamon

1 cup (113 g) grated sharp Cheddar cheese

8 strips bacon

4 large eggs

Kosher salt and ground black pepper

Set a small saucepan over medium-high heat and swirl in the oil. Add the onion and cook until it starts to turn translucent, 2 to 3 minutes. Add the water and oatmeal and bring to a boil. Reduce the heat, cover, and simmer for about 5 minutes, stirring occasionally, until the oats are cooked to your preferred consistency. Stir in the cheese and heat just enough to keep warm.

Meanwhile, set a large skillet over high heat. Working in two batches, add the bacon and fry until crisp, about 5 minutes, turning once. Transfer to a paper-towel–lined plate and crumble the bacon. Discard the bacon grease, reserving 1 tablespoon in the skillet.

Reheat the skillet over medium heat. Add the eggs to the skillet one at a time, being careful to keep the whites from overlapping too much. Cook undisturbed until the whites turn opaque, about 1 minute. Reduce the heat slightly, cover, and cook for about 4 minutes, or until the whites are completely set but the yolks are still soft. (For medium yolks, cook for 5 minutes; for hard yolks, cook for 6 minutes.)

Divide the oatmeal, bacon, and fried eggs among 4 bowls and season with salt and pepper to taste.

SAVORY PANCAKES WITH SCALLIONS, MUSHROOMS, AND GOAT CHEESE

Who says pancakes have to be sweet? Savory stacks are a surprising offering among the usual sweet treats of breakfast foods, and they seamlessly move into breakfast-for-dinner territory too. It all starts with my baking mix and the rest is up to your imagination. Swap the mushrooms for sun-dried tomatoes or forgo the goat cheese and melt Cheddar into the batter for oozy goodness. If breakfast is a big, fun, and boisterous tradition at your campsite, you can even host a "pancake bar" and offer a variety of add-ins (both sweet and savory) so friends can fill and flip their own.

MAKES 4 SERVINGS

FOR THE FILLING

4 medium cremini mushrooms, finely chopped

4 scallions, finely chopped

2 tablespoons olive oil

1 tablespoon chopped fresh thyme

½ teaspoon kosher salt

¼ teaspoon ground black pepper

FOR THE PANCAKES

2 cups (240 g) Multipurpose Baking Mix (page 32)

1½ cups (350 ml) milk

2 large eggs

Butter

Goat cheese

To make the filling, in a small bowl, combine the mushrooms, scallions, oil, thyme, salt, and pepper and set aside.

To make the pancakes, in a large bowl, whisk the baking mix with the milk and eggs until well blended.

Heat a large skillet over medium heat and melt a pat of butter, swirling to coat the surface. Ladle ¼ cup (60 ml) batter at a time into the skillet. Sprinkle 2 heaping tablespoons of the mushroom and scallion mixture over the batter and lightly press it into the pancake as it cooks. Cook until the edges begin to set, about 3 minutes. Flip the pancake and cook the other side until golden brown and completely set, about 2 minutes more.

Serve with a generous pat of butter and a dollop of goat cheese on top.

 USE IT UP

Where else can you use thyme if you have to buy a whole bunch of it? Put it in Whole Grilled Trout with Blood Orange and Fennel (page 89), Seared Rib-Eye Steaks with Herbed Board Sauce (page 91), Grilled Pork Medallions with Cherry-Bourbon Sauce (page 154), or Cedar-Planked Tomatoes Stuffed with Mushrooms and Gruyère (page 205).

BUTTERMILK PANCAKES WITH MAPLE, MASCARPONE, AND BERRIES

Pancakes are a much-loved morning ritual at camp (heck, even at home), but over the years I've seen far too many mixes come out of a box or even a spray can. Pancake mix is one of those things that's just too easy not to make at home, so stir up a batch of my baking mix and treat your tentmates to real, homemade, fresh, and fluffy buttermilk pancakes.

MAKES 4 SERVINGS

FOR THE PANCAKES

2 cups (240 g) Multipurpose Baking Mix (page 32)

2 cups (475 ml) buttermilk

½ cup (115 g) mascarpone cheese

2 large eggs

Butter

FOR THE TOPPINGS

2 tablespoons powdered sugar

½ cup (115 g) mascarpone cheese

2 cups (150 g) raspberries, blackberries, or blueberries

Maple syrup

To make the pancakes, in a large bowl, whisk together the baking mix, buttermilk, mascarpone, and eggs until well blended.

In a small bowl, stir the powdered sugar into the other ½ cup (115 g) of mascarpone and set aside.

Heat a large skillet over medium heat and melt a pat of butter, swirling to coat the surface. Ladle ¼ cup (60 ml) batter at a time into the skillet. Cook until bubbles break on the surface and the edges of the pancake begin to set, about 3 minutes. Flip and cook the other side until golden brown and completely set, about 2 minutes more. Repeat with the remaining batter. (To keep the pancakes warm, stack and wrap them in foil as they finish cooking.)

Serve with a dollop of the sweetened mascarpone, a handful of berries, and a drizzle of maple syrup on top.

SKEWERS:
TO SOAK OR NOT
TO SOAK?

Conventional culinary wisdom says that wooden skewers should be soaked in water before grilling. But does this really help prevent burning? We feel this practice is up for debate—it seems that no matter how long you soak the skewers, the ends are bound to scorch a bit over a hot grill. If you're concerned about the ends of your skewers burning off completely, you can wrap them in foil or, better yet, invest in stainless steel skewers.

GRILLED FRENCH TOAST AND BACON BITES

These breakfast kebabs are a fun take on the traditional French toast and bacon pairing. If your grill is big enough, you can even make French toast for a crowd by doubling the recipe. (Just be sure to bring enough skewers!) Make them a couple of days into your camping trip to give your bread some time to stale. If you're starting with fresh bread but want to make French toast in the morning, cut it the night before and lay the slices out to dry someplace warm and protected, like the dashboard of your car. The bread will lose just enough moisture for the ideal French toast texture.

MAKES 4 SERVINGS

3 large eggs

1 cup (240 ml) half-and-half or milk

¼ cup (60 ml) spiced rum

1 tablespoon sugar

6 (¾- to 1-inch-thick) slices slightly stale challah, brioche, or country-style bread

8 strips thick-cut bacon

Maple syrup

RECIPE NOTE

If you like your bacon smoky and sweet, brush on some maple syrup before grilling, and occasionally brush the slices with more syrup as they cook.

Prepare a grill for two-zone heat (see page 13).

In a wide, shallow dish, whisk together the eggs, half-and-half, rum, and sugar until the custard is very well blended. (You want to avoid any lingering clumps of egg yolk or egg white that will turn into cooked eggs on your French toast.)

Set aside 6 skewers until ready to use. Cut each slice of bread into 1-inch (2.5-cm) chunks. (You should have about 36 pieces.) Arrange the chunks in a single layer in the dish, working in batches if necessary, and soak the bread in the custard for about 10 seconds. Flip and soak the other side for about 10 seconds more until the bread is fully saturated but not falling apart. Thread the bread onto skewers and set aside to drain slightly. Thread the bacon onto the remaining skewers, folding the bacon back and forth accordion-style and piercing through the meaty parts of the bacon rather than the fat.

Grill the bacon over indirect heat, turning occasionally, for 10 to 12 minutes, until the edges are crisp and browned but the centers are still moist.

Grill the bread over direct heat, turning occasionally, for about 5 minutes, or until the surface is dry and golden brown and the centers are cooked through. If the bread is browning too quickly, finish the skewers over indirect heat once they get a good char.

Serve with a drizzle of maple syrup.

PEANUT BUTTER–STUFFED FRENCH TOAST WITH HONEYED BLACKBERRIES

French toast is already a decadent option for the first meal of the day, so why not make it even more decadent? This recipe is almost like a PB&J for breakfast, with swirls of peanut butter slathered between two thick slices of eggy bread and served with a syrupy, jammy topping of honey-sweetened berries. Feel free to sub in your favorite nut butter in place of the peanut butter and switch up the berries for some variation.

MAKES 4 SERVINGS

FOR THE TOPPING

3 cups (360 g) blackberries

¼ cup (60 ml) honey

Juice of ½ medium lemon

FOR THE FRENCH TOAST

3 large eggs

1 cup (240 ml) half-and-half or milk

1 tablespoon sugar

½ to ¾ cup (125 to 200 g) peanut butter

8 (¾- to 1-inch-thick) slices slightly stale challah, brioche, or country-style bread

1 tablespoon butter

To make the topping, in a small saucepan over medium-high heat, combine the blackberries, honey, and lemon juice. Cook until the berries begin to bubble and break down, about 5 minutes, stirring frequently to prevent the mixture from boiling over. Remove the pot from the heat and cover to keep warm.

To make the French toast, whisk together the eggs, half-and-half, and sugar in a wide, shallow dish until the custard is very well blended. (You want to avoid any lingering clumps of egg yolk or egg white that will turn into cooked eggs on your French toast.) Spread the peanut butter evenly over 4 slices of the bread, then top with the remaining 4 slices. Soak the sandwiches in the custard for about 10 seconds on each side, then set them aside to drain slightly.

In a large skillet over medium heat, melt the butter and swirl to completely coat the surface. Lay the sandwiches in the skillet and cook until the bottoms are golden, 3 to 4 minutes. Flip and cook for 3 to 4 minutes more, until both sides are crisp and browned.

Spoon the warm berries and their juices on top before serving.

✧ MIX IT UP ✧

To take your French toast up a level, start with exceptional bread. While the dense crumb of challah makes it many a cook's favorite, you can also try a French baguette, sourdough loaf, Italian panettone bread, or even cinnamon swirl bread. (Just omit the sugar in the custard if you start with a sweet bread.) Buy a whole loaf rather than a pre-sliced one so you can cut thicker slices yourself.

BREAKFAST BURRITOS AND LOX

There are bagels and lox. Then there are breakfast burritos and lox, a mashup of my favorite food vessel, the ever-versatile tortilla wrap, with the classic combo beloved by New Yorkers and commuters everywhere. If you're on the move in the morning, wrap these burritos in foil to keep them warm and enjoy them en route to your destination. (Or even at your destination—the burritos can be eaten up to 2 hours after they're made.)

MAKES 4 BURRITOS

8 large eggs

¼ cup (60 ml) milk

¼ teaspoon kosher salt

1 tablespoon olive oil, plus more for toasting

½ medium red onion, chopped

2 medium tomatoes, diced and drained

2 tablespoons capers, drained and chopped

3 ounces (85 g) smoked salmon, chopped

½ cup (113 g) cream cheese, softened (preferably dill cream cheese)

4 (10-inch) flour tortillas

Ground black pepper

In a large bowl, whisk together the eggs, milk, and salt until well blended.

Drizzle the oil in a large skillet over medium heat. Add the onion and cook until it starts to turn translucent, about 3 minutes. Add the egg mixture and cook undisturbed until it begins to set, about 2 minutes. Softly scramble the eggs until there's no longer liquid but they still look wet. Stir in the tomato, capers, and salmon and remove the skillet from the heat.

Spread 2 tablespoons of the cream cheese down the center of each tortilla. Spoon the egg mixture over the cream cheese, dividing it evenly among the tortillas, and scatter a pinch of pepper on top. Fold the sides of the tortillas up and over the mixture, then roll into burritos.

As an optional (but recommended) last step to warm and seal the burritos, wipe out the skillet with paper towels (or use a separate clean skillet) and heat over medium heat. Swirl in a little oil and arrange the burritos seam sides down in the skillet. Toast until golden brown, about 5 minutes, turning once.

FOOD ANTHROPOLOGY

Today, what most people refer to as lox (as in "bagels and lox") is actually Nova smoked salmon, the version commonly found in supermarkets. Also called Nova lox, Nova Scotia salmon, or simply smoked salmon (a generic term that can refer to any type of preparation), it's typically a fillet that is lightly cold-smoked after curing. The traditional Jewish brined salmon from where bagels and lox originated is actually made from the belly of salmon and has a saltier and bolder flavor.

TEX-MEX SCRAMBLED EGGS WITH TORTILLA CHIPS, TOMATOES, AND CHILES

Two things make this recipe especially good. First, it's considered a hangover cure (or maybe it's just the easiest meal to make after a late night of whiskey-fueled stories around a campfire). Second, it happens to be a brilliant way to use up those bits of broken chips at the bottom of the bag. Better known as migas (though not the migas of Spanish origin, which is a significantly different dish), this Tex-Mex version is essentially a scramble with a kick. Eat it as is, wrap it up in tortillas, or serve it with a side of refried beans for a more belly-filling meal.

MAKES 4 SERVINGS

8 large eggs

¼ cup (60 ml) milk

¼ teaspoon kosher salt, plus more for seasoning

1 cup (113 g) shredded Monterey jack, pepper jack, or sharp Cheddar cheese, divided

2 tablespoons olive oil

1 small yellow onion, finely chopped

4 cloves garlic, minced

1 poblano pepper, finely chopped

2 jalapeño peppers, minced

4 cups (120 g) corn tortilla chips, broken into 1-inch (2.5 cm) pieces, divided

2 medium tomatoes, finely chopped and drained

Ground black pepper

Handful of cilantro leaves, chopped

1 medium avocado, pitted, peeled, and sliced

Hot sauce

In a medium bowl, whisk together the eggs, milk, and salt until well blended. Stir in ½ cup (56 g) of the cheese and set aside.

In a large skillet over medium-high heat, add the oil, onion, and garlic and cook until the onion starts to turn translucent, 2 to 3 minutes. Add the poblano and jalapeño peppers and cook until tender, about 2 minutes.

Reduce the heat to medium-low and pour in the egg mixture. Scramble until curds start to form, about 3 minutes. Add two-thirds of the tortilla chips, gently stir to combine, and continue scrambling until the eggs are soft but still wet, about 3 minutes. Add the tomatoes and remaining ½ cup (56 g) cheese and cook until the eggs are softly scrambled and cooked through, about 3 minutes more. Stir in the remaining one-third tortilla chips and remove from the heat.

Season with salt and pepper to taste, garnish with cilantro, and serve with avocado and hot sauce on the side.

✧ MIX IT UP ✧

Migas makes a great lazy-morning breakfast, as everyone can choose and add his or her own accompaniments for the scramble. Set out a few options such as salsa, pico de gallo, scallions, guacamole, sour cream, corn or flour tortillas, refried beans, black beans, pinto beans, and more cheese.

SWEET POTATO, APPLE, AND PANCETTA HASH

This autumn-inspired breakfast adds a little flair to the basic bacon-and-potato hash by marrying pancetta and sweet potatoes for a dish that's deeper yet more delicate in flavor. You can vary the texture and taste by experimenting with different varieties of sweet potatoes (such as Japanese sweet potatoes, which have hints of chestnut) and apples (ranging from sweet to tart). To make more servings (or if you just really like eggs), simply make more wells in the final step of the recipe.

MAKES 4 SERVINGS

6 ounces pancetta, cut into small dice

1 small yellow onion, finely chopped

2 medium apples, cored and cut into ½-inch (1-cm) dice (about 1 pound/450 g)

2 tablespoons olive oil

2 large sweet potatoes, peeled and cut into ½-inch (1-cm) dice (about 2½ pounds/1 kg)

1 teaspoon red pepper flakes

½ teaspoon kosher salt

¼ teaspoon ground black pepper

2 cups (65 g) packed baby spinach

4 large eggs

RECIPE NOTE
In a well-stocked supermarket, pancetta can be found pre-diced and packaged in the cured meats cooler.

Heat a large skillet over medium-high heat. Add the pancetta and cook until browned and crispy, 5 to 8 minutes, stirring occasionally. Transfer the pancetta to a large plate, reserving the fat in the skillet.

Let the fat reheat for about 1 minute. Add the onion and cook until it starts to turn translucent, 2 to 3 minutes. Stir in the apples and cook until golden brown, 3 to 5 minutes. Transfer the onion and apples to the plate of pancetta.

Reheat the skillet and lightly coat the bottom with the oil. Add the sweet potatoes in a single layer and cook undisturbed until browned on the bottom, about 5 minutes. Sprinkle the red pepper flakes, salt, and pepper on top and continue cooking, stirring occasionally, for 8 to 10 minutes, or until the sweet potatoes are tender.

Return the pancetta, onion, and apples to the skillet and stir to combine. Add the spinach and cook until wilted, 2 to 3 minutes.

Using a spoon, make 4 deep wells in the mixture. Crack an egg into each well, cover the skillet, and cook until the yolks are just set, 8 to 10 minutes. (If you like your yolks less runny, poach for a few additional minutes.)

BACON-WRAPPED POTATOES WITH BLUE CHEESE

There's always that one person in camp who loves to wake with the sun, start the coffee, and slowly rouse the others from their tents with the smell of bacon wafting through the air. If that person is you, put these potatoes on the menu. They take a little longer to cook but only a few minutes to assemble, making them the perfect lazy-morning meditation. Serve them as a whole meal in themselves or as a side dish to eggs (and don't stop at breakfast, either—they go great with steaks for dinner).

MAKES 4 SERVINGS

Olive oil spray

6 strips bacon, cut in half

12 new potatoes (about 1½ pounds/680 g)

Ground black pepper

1 cup (227 g) sour cream

½ cup (56 g) crumbled blue cheese

2 scallions, thinly sliced

Milk (optional)

Prepare a mound of wood coals, hardwood lump charcoal, or charcoal briquettes (see page 12). Move about a quart's worth of coals to the cooking pit and arrange them in a ring (see page 120).

Lightly spray a dutch oven with oil. Wrap a strip of bacon tightly around each potato and arrange the wrapped potatoes in a single layer in the oven, bacon seams down. Scatter a few pinches of pepper on top, cover, and place 2 rings of coals on the lid.

Roast over high heat for 40 to 50 minutes, until the bacon is crisp and the potatoes are tender. Replenish the coals as needed to maintain high heat and rotate the oven and lid halfway through for even cooking.

In a medium bowl, combine the sour cream, blue cheese, and scallions. If desired, add a little milk to thin the consistency. Serve as a dip or drizzle for the potatoes.

HOW DID THE DUTCH OVEN
GET ITS NAME?

The term *dutch oven* has endured since the early 1700s, though its origin is somewhat of a mystery. It's commonly believed that an Englishman named Abraham Darby traveled to the Netherlands to study the more advanced Dutch process for casting metal cooking vessels. He returned to Britain and eventually developed and patented a superior method that produced thinner and lighter pots than their predecessors. It's possible his "dutch ovens" may have been named for the original Dutch process.

Another theory proposes that the name came from Dutch salesmen who brought their cast metal pots to the American colonies, and yet another suggests the name arose from the pots' popularity among the early "Dutch" (German) settlers of Pennsylvania—*Dutch* being an adaptation of the German word *Deutsch*.

DUTCH OVEN SPINACH AND ARTICHOKE FRITTATA

Frittatas are one of those meals I affectionately call "kitchen pantry" dishes, as you can add almost anything from your kitchen (pantry or not) to a custardlike base of eggs. While traditional frittatas require flipping (or starting on the stove and finishing in the oven), a dutch oven frittata is a one-pot wonder, cooking in the same vessel, same spot. Spinach and artichokes are a classic pairing, but dig through your cooler for other add-ins that may be languishing at the end of your camping trip. Last night's leftover sausage, half an avocado, some sprigs of basil, and the odds and ends from cans and jars are all fair game.

MAKES 4 SERVINGS

12 large eggs

½ cup (120 ml) milk

½ cup (56 g) shredded sharp Cheddar cheese

½ teaspoon kosher salt

Olive oil spray

2 medium shallots, sliced

4 cloves garlic, minced

3 cups (300 g) packed baby spinach

1 (14-ounce/400 g) can artichoke hearts, drained and chopped

½ cup (50 g) grated Parmesan cheese

Prepare a mound of wood coals, hardwood lump charcoal, or charcoal briquettes (see page 12). Move about half the coals to the cooking pit and arrange them in a full spread (see page 120).

In a large bowl, lightly beat the eggs with the milk, Cheddar, and salt.

Spray a dutch oven with oil and heat it over the coals. Add the shallots and garlic to the oven and cook until the shallots start to turn translucent, about 2 minutes. Stir in the spinach and cook until wilted, 2 to 3 minutes. Add the artichokes and stir to combine.

Move the oven off the coals and arrange the coals in a ring (see page 120). Set the oven on the coals, pour the egg mixture evenly over the vegetables, and give a quick stir to incorporate all of the ingredients. Cook undisturbed until the eggs start to set around the edges, 3 to 5 minutes. Sprinkle the Parmesan on top, cover, and place 1½ rings of coals on the lid.

Bake over medium heat until the eggs are puffy and the frittata jiggles slightly when you push on it, about 15 minutes.

Remove the oven from the heat, uncover, and let stand for 5 minutes before serving.

CHAPTER 3

FEASTING ... OVER THE FIRE

Cooking in a fire pit is as primitive and thrilling as it gets. You're closer to the fire, you're at the mercy of the weather, and your family and friends are gathered around for the show. Even if you end up burning dinner—and you probably will at some point, as all great grill masters have—it's still a good time for all. And this is exactly why fire pits are such an appealing entry to the world of live-fire cooking.

With nothing between you and the flames (well, maybe just a cooking grate), food becomes an adventure—buried in the ashes, singed on the coals, or seared over hot metal. The interactive nature of cooking over fire will make even those ordinary weeknight meals something to look forward to.

BUILD YOUR OWN NO-FRILLS FIRE PIT

There are many ways to build a fire pit, but this foundational design is easily replicated with inexpensive materials found at your local home improvement store. It can also be started and finished in a single afternoon so you can get grilling the same night!

BEFORE YOU BEGIN

+ Check local building codes and ordinances as well as neighborhood covenants, conditions, and restrictions to confirm fire pits are allowed on your property.

+ Find out what the required setbacks are from structures and property lines.

+ Think about how the prevailing winds blow through your yard and place your fire pit in a spot where smoke won't be blowing into your windows.

+ Choose a solid, level, and open area away from your house and any low-hanging limbs or other combustible objects.

+ Leave enough space around the fire pit—at least 6 feet (180 cm)—from the fire pit to the back legs of your furniture to set up seating comfortably.

DETAILS

This fire pit measures 44 inches (110 cm) in outside diameter, 32 inches (80 cm) in inside diameter, and 15 inches (37.5 cm) in height. If you decide to use different materials, construct your fire pit to a final size between 36 and 44 inches (90 and 110 cm) in diameter, which creates enough room for a good fire but still keeps gatherers close enough to chat.

MATERIALS NEEDED

+ 48 (4 x 11.6 inch, or 10 x 29.5 cm) flagstone retaining wall blocks
+ Lava rocks, gravel, or sand

Step 1: Clear and level the ground of grass, weeds, rocks, and other debris down to the bare dirt. Rake it smooth and tamp down on the dirt to compact it as much as possible. Level it again to make sure your fire pit doesn't turn out lopsided.

Step 2: Set the first layer of the fire pit by arranging 12 blocks in a ring. Every other block, leave a small gap about 2 inches (5 cm) wide to allow for proper airflow.

Step 3: Continue laying the blocks in a ring, using 12 blocks per layer and staggering the joints for structural support. Gradually tighten the size of the gaps as you build up the layers until the top (and last) layer of blocks is fully touching with no gaps.

Step 1

Step 2

Steps 3 and 4

Step 4: Cover the bottom of the fire pit with a 4-inch (10 cm) base of lava rocks, gravel, or sand to help provide drainage. While you can certainly make a fire over dirt, having drainage allows your fire pit to always be ready for use. Otherwise, you may find it full of dirty ash water a day or two after it rains. I also like to cover the ground surrounding the fire pit with the same rock or gravel, which helps keep dust down and prevent the fire from accidentally spreading.

Step 5: Light your first fire, kick back, and relax! (See page 10 for more on starting and managing the fire.)

PEPPERCORN-CRUSTED CAVEMAN STEAK WITH HORSERADISH CREAM

It seems fitting that an outdoor-themed cookbook should include the most primal of cooking methods, one in which nothing more is needed than a blazing hot bed of coals. It also makes for a great party trick: "Hey, what's for dinner tonight?" "This!"—fling steak into the fire pit.

Caveman steak, also known as Eisenhower steak, was popularized by President Dwight D. Eisenhower, who loved a hefty sirloin cooked right on the fire. No, not over it—right on it. The searing heat gave the steak a beautiful charred crust while the interior stayed rosy and juicy. Many decades later, it remains a fun, simple, and showstopping way to grill for a crowd. Though it might seem contrary, the steaks—amazingly—don't incinerate into ash and they produce none of the sooty flare-up common when cooking on a grate above the coals.

I like to use porterhouse or T-bone for this recipe because the large bone and thick slab of meat look impressive in the fire, but any cut will work. Try this method with flat iron, rib eye, or even pork or lamb chops. The magic number to get a good char on the outside with medium-rare on the inside is a 1½- to 2-inch (3.5 to 5 cm)-thick steak. If you don't have a very hot-burning hardwood such as oak or apple, I recommend using hardwood lump charcoal to ensure maximum heat output from your coals.

MAKES 4 SERVINGS

FOR THE STEAK

2 tablespoons (17 g) peppercorns

2 (27-ounce, or 762 g; 1½ to 2 inches, or 3.5 to 5 cm, thick) porterhouse steaks

Kosher salt

FOR THE HORSERADISH CREAM

½ cup (115 g) sour cream

2 tablespoons (30 g) prepared grated horseradish, drained

1 tablespoon (3 g) minced fresh chives

1 teaspoon distilled white wine vinegar

¼ teaspoon kosher salt, plus more as needed

Pinch ground black pepper, plus more as needed

Heavy cream, for thinning (optional)

RECIPE CONTINUES

HOT TIP

When I want medium-rare on thicker cuts such as porterhouse, I take my steaks off the grill at 120°F (49°C) so they'll reach my desired serving temperature of 125°F to 130°F (52°C to 54.5°C) while they rest. (See pages 20 and 21 for a grilling temperature chart and how to account for carryover cooking.)

Prepare a hot single-level fire in a fire pit (see page 13).

To make the steak: Crack the peppercorns into rough halves and quarters. (I like to use the bottom of a cast iron skillet for this, but you can also use a pepper grinder on the coarsest setting, a mortar with a pestle, or a mallet.) Generously season the steaks on both sides with the cracked pepper and salt.

Spread the coals into a flat, uniform bed at least 2 inches (5 cm) deep. Briefly fan them with a rolled-up newspaper to disperse excess ash.

Place the steaks directly on the coals. Grill, undisturbed, for 4 to 5 minutes. Flip the steaks and grill for 4 to 5 minutes more, until an instant-read thermometer inserted into the center of the meat registers 120°F (49°C), for medium-rare.

Using tongs, lift the steaks and tap the tongs against the side of the grill to knock off any clinging embers. If you have some ash, flick it off with a pastry brush. Transfer the steaks to a sheet pan, tent with aluminum foil, and let rest for 10 minutes while you prepare the horseradish cream.

To make the horseradish cream: In a small bowl, whisk all the cream ingredients until combined. Taste and add more salt or pepper, as desired. For a thinner sauce that you can drizzle on the steaks, whisk in a bit of heavy cream to reach a pourable consistency you like.

To serve, cut each section of meat (the strip steak and the tenderloin steak) from the bone. Slice the steaks perpendicular to the bone and serve with a dollop of horseradish cream.

EMBER-ROASTED BEET SALAD WITH ORANGE, FENNEL, AND FETA

I admit: the first time I threw a whole vegetable into a fire pit, I was terrified. Pulling out a crispy blackened beet from the embers had me convinced I'd ruined dinner. But underneath the ashy-burnt exterior was a beet so sweet and tender, its golden flesh tinged with a hint of wood smoke, I realized roasting in embers was a remarkably forgiving method.

Tough-skinned beets (much like acorn squash on page 68) can truly take the heat; their flavor only intensifies when pitched into the coals. This leaves the grill grate free to cook other things, if you wish, with the beets roasting underneath them. Just remember to give them a spin every so often to achieve a deep, all-over char—a sign of good food to come.

MAKES 4 TO 6 SERVINGS

4 beets (preferably golden or Chioggia, about 2 pounds, or 908 g, total), unpeeled, greens trimmed

¼ cup (60 ml) olive oil

1 tablespoon (15 ml) balsamic vinegar

¼ teaspoon kosher salt

Pinch ground black pepper

1 fennel bulb, trimmed, cored, quartered, and thinly sliced

1 shallot, thinly sliced

4 oranges (preferably a mix of navel and blood oranges)

¼ cup (37.5 g) crumbled feta cheese

¼ cup (30 g) chopped walnuts

Prepare a hot single-level fire in a fire pit (see page 13) and spread the coals into a flat, uniform bed at least 2 inches (5 cm) deep. Keep a small fire going in the back of the fire pit to replenish the coals, as needed.

Place the beets directly on the coals. Roast for about 45 minutes, turning every 10 to 15 minutes, until the skin is evenly charred and the flesh is easily pierced with a skewer. Transfer the beets to a cutting board and let cool.

Meanwhile, make the dressing. In a bowl large enough to hold the salad, whisk the olive oil, vinegar, salt, and pepper. Set aside.

When the beets are cool enough to handle, using a paring knife, slice the skins off the beets. Cut the beets into ½-inch (1 cm) wedges. Add the beets, fennel, and shallot to the bowl with the dressing and toss to coat.

Slice the peel and pith off the oranges. Cut them crosswise into ¼-inch (0.6 cm) wheels. Divide the orange wheels among four plates. Heap equal amounts of the beet and fennel mixture on top. Sprinkle the feta and walnuts evenly over each salad.

TO WRAP OR NOT TO WRAP?

With burly vegetables such as beets (as well as potatoes and sweet potatoes), I like to throw them into the embers as is. Having direct contact with the coals and letting the skins char helps develop the flavors more deeply. That said, you can wrap your vegetables in heavy-duty aluminum foil before cooking them in the coals. It's only necessary if you want to preserve and eat the skins (in the case of baked potatoes) or you don't want to deal with the mess of peeling them.

SMOKY EMBER-ROASTED EGGPLANT DIP

If you like baba ghanoush, you'll love this campfire take on the classic Mediterranean dip. The embers add a smoky depth of flavor you simply can't replicate in the oven. When nestled in the coals, the eggplants blister and blacken to the point where they almost look carbonized. But once you open them, you'll find flesh that's supple, savory, and almost meaty. They are just as good eaten like this, perhaps with a spicy tomato sauce slathered on top, or puréed into a smoke-kissed dip you can serve with grilled flatbread or baguette.

MAKES 3 TO 4 CUPS (750 G TO 1 KG)

3 globe eggplants (about 3 pounds, or 1.35 kg, total)

1 red onion, unpeeled

2 garlic cloves, chopped

¼ cup (60 ml) olive oil, plus more for drizzling

¾ teaspoon kosher salt, plus more for seasoning

¼ cup (60 g) tahini

2 tablespoons (30 ml) fresh lemon juice

¼ teaspoon ground cumin

Handful minced fresh parsley, plus more for garnishing

Smoked paprika, for garnishing

Prepare a hot single-level fire in a fire pit (see page 13) and spread the coals into a flat, uniform bed at least 2 inches (5 cm) deep.

Prick the eggplants in several places with a fork.

Place the eggplants and red onion directly on the coals. Grill, turning occasionally, until the eggplants have collapsed, their flesh is very soft, and the skins are charred all over, about 20 minutes for the eggplants and 30 minutes for the onion. Transfer the vegetables to a cutting board and let cool.

Halve the eggplants lengthwise. Scoop out the flesh and place it in a mesh strainer. (It's fine to leave some of the burnt bits on, as they add flavor.) Let drain for at least 15 minutes, mashing the flesh with the back of a spoon as needed to release excess liquid.

Meanwhile, trim and peel the onion. Coarsely chop it and transfer to a food processor. Add the garlic, olive oil, and salt. Pulse into a chunky purée. Add the eggplant, tahini, lemon juice, and cumin. Pulse until the ingredients are combined but still have some texture. Taste and add more salt, as desired.

Transfer the baba ghanoush to a medium bowl and stir in the parsley. Drizzle with a little olive oil, sprinkle a pinch of paprika on top, and garnish with parsley before serving.

WHAT ELSE CAN YOU COOK IN THE EMBERS?

Most self-contained vegetables that have a good amount of moisture inside are ideal candidates for the low and slow method of roasting in ashes, particularly if they're buried under a fire. Think garlic, potatoes, sweet potatoes, and winter squash.

Other vegetables with a sacrificial layer that can be stripped away before eating do well when cooked on top of the coals. Try artichokes, beets, cabbage, eggplant, fennel, leeks, onion, sweet and hot peppers, and sweet corn.

Smaller, more delicate vegetables that need only a kiss of smoke and a blast of heat benefit from a quick sear on the coals to intensify their flavor, such as asparagus and shishito and Pa- drón peppers.

COAL-BLISTERED SHISHITO PEPPERS

Shishito peppers are like the Russian roulette of the food world—mostly mild in flavor, but, every few peppers, you might bite into one that sets your taste buds on fire! Along with their Spanish counterpart, Padrón peppers, shishitos are ideal for ember grilling because their thin skins mean they cook quickly and require no peeling. They make an easy and addictive appetizer while you prep the main course (perhaps the Peppercorn-Crusted Caveman Steak, page 58) or a quick side dish after you take the meat off the coals.

MAKES 4 SERVINGS

1 pound (454 g) shishito peppers

4 teaspoons (20 ml) soy sauce

2 teaspoons toasted sesame oil

Kosher salt

Prepare a hot single-level fire in a fire pit (see page 13). Spread the coals into a flat, uniform bed at least 2 inches (5 cm) deep. Briefly fan them with a rolled-up newspaper to disperse excess ash.

Arrange the peppers directly on the coals. Grill until charred all over, 3 to 4 minutes, turning frequently. Transfer the peppers to a sheet pan.

Drizzle with the soy sauce and sesame oil and toss to coat. Serve with a sprinkle of salt on top.

GRILLED BRIE WITH SWEET CHERRY SAUCE

If you need a quick and easy appetizer for your next gathering, this melt-in-your-mouth Brie is certain to elevate your cheese board. It works well with other fruits, too, like blueberries, blackberries, and figs. Serve it with grilled or toasted baguette, artisan crackers, and olives for a well-rounded party spread.

MAKES 4 SERVINGS

1 tablespoon (14 g) butter

1 cup (155 g) pitted, halved sweet cherries

1 teaspoon thinly sliced fresh basil

1 (8-ounce, or 225 g) wheel Brie cheese

Olive oil cooking spray, for cooking the Brie

Kosher salt

Honey, for serving

Grilled baguette slices, for serving

Prepare a medium-hot single-level fire in a fire pit (see page 13) with a grill grate over the coals.

On the stovetop, in a medium saucepan over medium heat, melt the butter. Add the cherries. Cook for 5 to 7 minutes, until they begin to break down and release their juices, stirring occasionally. Remove from the heat, stir in the basil, and keep warm.

Lightly spray the Brie rind with cooking spray and sprinkle with a pinch of salt.

Place the Brie on the grate, oiled-side down, and grill, undisturbed, for about 2 minutes. Lightly spray the top of the Brie with cooking spray, gently turn it over (being careful not to break it open), and grill for about 2 minutes, until it feels soft and gooey inside and there are good grill marks on both sides.

Transfer the Brie to a plate and top with the cherry sauce. Drizzle with honey and serve alongside grilled baguette slices.

EMBER-ROASTED ACORN SQUASH WITH CHARRED POBLANOS, COTIJA, AND CREMA

With their thick burly skins, acorn squash are perfectly suited for ember grilling. They roast right in their own shells while retaining their moisture and infusing with the lovely aroma of wood smoke. The result is a squash so buttery you can slice it open and eat it with a spoon! Any winter squash will work for this recipe, including kabocha, kuri, butternut, or plain ol' pumpkin. If you like a spicier kick, throw another pepper into the embers to divvy up among the squash bowls.

MAKES 4 SERVINGS

2 (1-pound, or 454 g) acorn squash

4 poblano peppers

Kosher salt

Ground black pepper

⅓ to ½ cup (41 to 61 g) crumbled Cotija cheese

⅓ to ½ cup (80 to 120 ml) crema Mexicana

Finely chopped fresh cilantro, for garnishing

Prepare a hot single-level fire in a fire pit (see page 13) and spread the coals into a flat, uniform bed at least 2 inches (5 cm) deep. Keep a small fire going in the back of the fire pit to replenish the coals, as needed.

Nestle the squash into the coals. Roast for about 45 minutes, turning every 10 to 15 minutes, until the skin is evenly and lightly charred and the flesh is tender.

Arrange the peppers directly on the coals. Cook for about 10 minutes, until the skin is charred all over, turning occasionally. Remove the peppers from the heat and place them in a plastic bag. Let them sweat for 5 to 10 minutes. Transfer the peppers to a cutting board to cool. Peel and discard the skin. Halve the peppers lengthwise and remove the core and seeds. Chop the peppers into bite-size pieces. Cover to keep warm until the squash is done.

When a skewer easily pierces the thickest part of the squash, transfer them to a cutting board. Halve each squash lengthwise and scoop out and discard the seeds. Season to taste with salt and pepper and divide among four bowls.

Top each squash with an equal amount of peppers and cheese. Serve with a drizzle of crema and a sprinkle of cilantro.

CHARRED BEEFSTEAK TOMATOES WITH BASIL AND BURRATA

Caprese salads are a staple at many of my outdoor gatherings, and this version is a simple twist on a summer classic—hefty beefsteak tomatoes picked at the height of the season, seared on the grill, and paired with creamy burrata. The char adds a subtle fragrant smoke while retaining all the freshness of those lusciously ripe summer tomatoes.

MAKES 4 SERVINGS

2 (12-ounce, or 340 g) beefsteak tomatoes, halved lengthwise

Olive oil, for the tomatoes and dressing

Kosher salt

Ground black pepper

4 (4-ounce, or 115 g) balls burrata cheese

Balsamic vinegar, for dressing

Large handful fresh basil, thinly sliced

Prepare a hot single-level fire in a fire pit (see page 13) with a grill grate over the coals.

Drizzle the cut sides of the tomato halves with olive oil and sprinkle with salt and pepper.

Arrange the tomatoes, cut-side down, on the grate. Cook, undisturbed, for 3 to 4 minutes, until slashed with grill marks. (You only need to sear the surface of the tomatoes, not cook them all the way through.)

Tear each burrata ball in half and divide among four plates. Arrange 1 tomato half next to the burrata and douse with a generous drizzle of olive oil and vinegar. (I like a 2-to-1 ratio of oil to vinegar.) Scatter basil on top and serve with a sprinkle of salt and pepper to taste.

GRILLED CUCUMBER DILL PICKLES

When it comes to pickles, I am all about refrigerator pickles (also called quick pickles) because they don't require any water bath canning or special equipment. You can repurpose any jar you have around and, within a matter of days, enjoy pickles that rival the ones you used to buy from the store!

Here, giving cucumbers a kiss of smoke on the grill before brining adds another flavor dimension to the traditional dill pickle. The key to crunchy pickles is grilling them just long enough to leave good grill marks, but not so long they turn soft.

MAKES 3 PINTS (ABOUT 900 G)

1½ cups (360 ml) water

1½ cups (360 ml) apple cider vinegar

2 tablespoons (25 g) sugar

2 tablespoons (36 g) kosher salt

1 teaspoon red pepper flakes

3 garlic cloves, thinly sliced

1½ pounds (681 g) Kirby (pickling) cucumbers, quartered lengthwise

1 yellow onion, cut crosswise into ½-inch (1 cm) rounds

Olive oil cooking spray, for preparing the vegetables

6 dill sprigs

Prepare a medium-hot single-level fire in a fire pit (see page 13) with a grill grate over the coals.

On the stovetop, in a small saucepan over medium heat, combine the water, vinegar, sugar, salt, red pepper flakes, and garlic. Stir until the salt dissolves. Remove the brine from the heat.

Lightly spray the cucumbers and onion with cooking spray and arrange them on the grate. Grill for 3 to 4 minutes per side, until good grill marks form.

Pack 3 quart- (960 ml)-size jars with equal amounts of cucumber, onion, and dill. Pour the brine over the vegetables, leaving about ½ inch (1 cm) of space from the top. Gently run a knife or chopstick around the inside perimeter of each jar to release trapped air bubbles and wipe the rims clean with a paper towel. Seal the jars and refrigerate for at least 3 days before eating. The pickles will keep, refrigerated, for up to 3 months, but will lose their crunch over time.

GET SAUCED

These pickles are the secret ingredient in my "special sauce," which I love to slather on homemade burgers and sandwiches: Kewpie mayonnaise, ketchup, and chopped grilled dill pickles. I don't have a recipe; I just eyeball the ingredients every time I make it, using a little more mayo than ketchup to achieve the right pale orange color, and enough pickles to give the sauce some punch.

Kewpie is a Japanese brand of mayo that's smoother and slightly sweeter than American mayo. Find it in Asian markets.

FOR THE SALAD

1 pound (454 g) mixed tomatoes

1 teaspoon kosher salt, plus more for seasoning

2 zucchini, halved lengthwise

2 bell peppers, any color or a mix, trimmed, cored, and halved lengthwise

1 globe eggplant, cut crosswise into 1-inch (2.5 cm) slices

1 red onion, cut crosswise into 1-inch (2.5 cm) slices

Olive oil cooking spray, for preparing the vegetables

Ground black pepper

1 loaf artisan bread, halved horizontally (as if for a large sandwich)

½ cup (18 g) packed fresh basil leaves, chopped

FOR THE DRESSING

½ cup (120 ml) olive oil

2 tablespoons (18 g) capers, drained

2 garlic cloves, minced

2 tablespoons (30 ml) red wine vinegar

1 tablespoon (15 g) Dijon mustard

½ teaspoon kosher salt

¼ teaspoon ground black pepper

GRILLED PANZANELLA

This Tuscan bread salad truly takes advantage of beautiful summer produce. While traditional panzanella is centered on the best tomatoes you can find, I like to mix it up with other nightshades—almost like a ratatouille in panzanella form.

MAKES 4 TO 6 SERVINGS

To make the salad: Prepare a medium-hot single-level fire in a fire pit (see page 13) with a grill grate over the coals.

Halve the tomatoes (if using cherry tomatoes) or cut into ½-inch (1 cm) wedges (if using slicing tomatoes). Place the tomatoes in a bowl large enough to hold the salad. Toss the tomatoes with the salt. Set aside.

Mist the zucchini, bell peppers, eggplant, and red onion with cooking spray. Season both sides with salt and pepper.

Arrange the vegetables on the grate. Grill for 4 to 6 minutes per side, until tender and lightly charred. Remove each vegetable as it's finished and transfer to a cutting board.

Mist both sides of the bread halves with cooking spray. Arrange the bread on the grate. Grill until brown and crispy, 30 seconds to 1 minute per side.

Chop the grilled vegetables into bite-size pieces and add them to the bowl of tomatoes.

Cut the bread into 1-inch (2.5 cm) chunks. Add 6 heaping cups (225 g) of bread along with the basil to the bowl and toss to combine. (Reserve any remaining bread for another use.)

To make the dressing: In a small bowl, whisk the olive oil, capers, garlic, vinegar, mustard, salt, and pepper until well blended. Pour three-fourths of the dressing over the salad and toss to coat. Let the salad sit for at least 15 minutes for the bread to soak up all the flavors from the dressing and vegetables. Taste and add more dressing, if desired.

FOR THE AVOCADO SPREAD

2 avocados, halved lengthwise and pitted

1 tomato, diced

2 garlic cloves, minced

Juice of 1 lime

Handful finely chopped fresh cilantro, plus more for garnishing

½ teaspoon kosher salt, plus more for seasoning

FOR THE SHRIMP

2 tablespoons (30 ml) olive oil

Juice of 1 lime

½ teaspoon ground cumin

½ teaspoon ground coriander

½ teaspoon red pepper flakes

1 pound (454 g) medium shrimp, peeled and deveined

Kosher salt

1 loaf artisan bread, cut into ½-inch (1 cm) slices

Olive oil cooking spray, for preparing the bread

SPICY GRILLED SHRIMP ON AVOCADO TOAST

Avocado toast has become very popular in casual cuisine, and I, too, am a fan! Somehow, this simple little concoction makes sense for any and every occasion: as a midday snack or happy hour nibble, assembled for brunch or devoured for dinner. When you top it with spicy grilled shrimp, it's the perfect summer nosh for feeding a crowd. Just add margaritas!

MAKES 4 SERVINGS

Prepare a medium-hot single-level fire in a fire pit (see page 13) with a grill grate over the coals.

To make the avocado spread: Scoop the avocado flesh into a medium bowl and smash it with a fork. Add the tomato, garlic, lime juice, cilantro, and salt. Stir to combine. Taste and add more salt, as desired. Set aside until the toasts are ready for assembly.

To make the shrimp: In a large bowl, whisk the olive oil, lime juice, cumin, coriander, and red pepper flakes until combined. Add the shrimp and toss to coat. Cover and refrigerate for 15 minutes (but no more than 30 minutes).

Lightly mist both sides of the bread slices with cooking spray. Arrange the bread on the grate. Grill for about 30 seconds per side, until toasted brown and lightly charred. Transfer the toasts to a sheet pan.

Thread the shrimp onto skewers and season both sides with salt.

Place the skewers on the grate. Grill for about 2 minutes per side, until the flesh is opaque and just cooked through. Pull the shrimp off the skewers and chop into bite-size pieces.

Top each toast slice with a thin layer of avocado spread and a few spoonfuls of shrimp. Garnish with cilantro and serve.

HOT TIP

If you have leftover bread at the end of the day, grill the slices and pulse them in a food processor to make grilled bread crumbs you can use in other recipes. Grilled bread crumbs can be frozen in an airtight container for up to 3 months.

FOR THE SALSA VERDE

1½ pounds (681 g) tomatillos, husked

1 white onion, halved lengthwise, root left intact, coarsely chopped

2 jalapeño peppers

Olive oil cooking spray, for preparing the vegetables

½ cup (8 g) packed fresh cilantro

Juice of 1 lime

½ teaspoon kosher salt, plus more as needed

FOR THE CHICKEN TACOS

2 tablespoons (12 g) cumin seeds, coarsely crushed

1 teaspoon kosher salt, plus more for seasoning

½ teaspoon ground black pepper, plus more for seasoning

2 pounds (908 g) boneless, skinless chicken thighs, trimmed of excess fat

2 red onions, quartered, roots left intact

Olive oil cooking spray, for preparing the onion

Warmed flour or corn tortillas, for serving

Toppings of choice (I recommend thinly sliced radishes, sliced avocado, and chopped fresh cilantro)

CUMIN-CRUSTED CHICKEN TACOS WITH SMOKY SALSA VERDE

When it comes to chicken, I'm all about the dark meat. It's more tender, more flavorful, and less likely to taste like cardboard from overcooking. Chicken thighs also cook quickly and take well to higher temperatures, making them ideal for weeknight grilling. Don't be shy with the cumin seasoning—the chicken can take it, and the tangy tomatillo salsa tempers the bold spice. You'll have enough salsa left to serve with tortilla chips!

MAKES 4 SERVINGS

Prepare a medium-hot two-zone fire in a fire pit (see page 13) with a grill grate over the coals.

To make the salsa verde: Mist the tomatillos, onion, and jalapeños with cooking spray. Arrange the vegetables on the grate over direct heat. Grill for about 8 minutes, until tender and charred, turning occasionally. Remove each vegetable as it's finished and transfer to a cutting board.

Trim and coarsely chop the grilled onion. Stem and core the grilled jalapeños.

In a food processor, combine the chopped onion and jalapeños, tomatillos, cilantro, lime juice, and salt. Pulse until the ingredients are combined into a sauce but still have a slightly chunky consistency. Taste and add more salt, if desired. Transfer to a small bowl. Set aside until ready to use. (The salsa can also be made up to 5 days in advance and refrigerated in an airtight container.)

To make the chicken tacos: In a small bowl, stir together the cumin seeds, salt, and pepper. Season the chicken on all sides with the spice mix.

Mist the red onions with cooking spray and season with a few pinches of salt and pepper.

RECIPE CONTINUES

Arrange the chicken and red onions on the grate over direct heat. Grill the chicken for 10 to 12 minutes, turning occasionally, until evenly charred on both sides and an instant-read thermometer inserted into the thickest part of the thigh reaches 180°F to 185°F (82°C to 85°C). (Move the chicken over indirect heat if it seems to be burning before it reaches temperature.) Grill the onions until tender and charred, about 8 minutes, turning occasionally.

Slice the chicken and trim and slice the onion.

Assemble a taco bar with the chicken, onions, tortillas, salsa verde, and toppings of choice. Invite guests to serve themselves.

GRILLED SKIRT STEAK TACOS WITH PICKLED RED ONIONS

Skirt steak has a lot of things going for it: rich, buttery, and beefy, robust enough to take a bold seasoning, and super easy to grill (even for first-timers). Because it's such a thin piece of meat, skirt steak can go from tender and juicy to tough as hell very quickly—so all it needs is a solid sear on the hottest part of the grill. This also makes it a great cut of steak to keep on hand when you want a fuss-free dinner that doesn't skimp on flavor.

MAKES 4 SERVINGS

Pickled Red Onions (recipe follows), for serving

2 teaspoons kosher salt

2 teaspoons ground cumin

1 teaspoon ground coriander

1 teaspoon ground black pepper

2 pounds (908 g) skirt steak (preferably outside skirt), trimmed of fat and halved

Warmed flour or corn tortillas, for serving

Lime wedges, for serving

More toppings of choice (I recommend thinly sliced jalapeños, finely chopped fresh cilantro, shredded lettuce, and crema Mexicana)

At least 1 hour before you plan to serve the tacos, make the pickled red onions.

Prepare a hot two-zone fire in a fire pit (see page 13) with a grill grate over the coals.

In a small bowl, stir together the salt, cumin, coriander, and pepper. Liberally season the steaks on both sides with the spice mix.

Arrange the steaks on the grate over direct heat. Grill for about 3 minutes per side, or until an instant-read thermometer inserted into the thickest part of the steak reads 130°F (54.5°C) for medium.

Remove the steaks from the heat and let rest for 5 minutes. For the most tender bites, slice each steak *with* the grain into 4-inch (10 cm) sections, then slice them *against* the grain into ¼-inch (0.6 cm) strips.

Serve with warmed tortillas, pickled red onions, lime wedges, and additional toppings of choice.

PICKLED RED ONIONS

MAKES 1 PINT (454 G)

½ cup (120 ml) water

½ cup (120 ml) apple cider vinegar

1 tablespoon (12.5 g) sugar

1 teaspoon kosher salt

1 red onion, very thinly sliced

In a small bowl, whisk the water, vinegar, sugar, and salt until the grains dissolve. Pack the onions into a pint-size (480 ml) jar. Pour the pickling brine over them. Using the back of a spoon, tamp down on the onions to submerge them fully in the brine. Let sit for at least 1 hour before serving. Refrigerate any unused pickles. They will keep, refrigerated, for up to 3 months.

GRILLED FINGERLING FRIES

These grilled "fries" are a favorite at our backyard barbecues because they go with just about anything—from burgers (pages 83 and 86) to seared steaks and spatchcocked chicken (page 141). I like to serve mine with garlicky melted butter, but they're also delicious with other dips and sauces, such as Avocado Aioli (page 202), Smoky Salsa Verde (page 78), or your go-to barbecue sauce.

MAKES 4 SERVINGS

1 pound (454 g) fingerling potatoes

1 teaspoon kosher salt, plus more for seasoning

3 tablespoons (42 g) butter

2 garlic cloves, minced

Olive oil, for drizzling

Ground black pepper

Handful grated Parmesan cheese

Handful finely chopped fresh parsley

Prepare a hot single-level fire in a fire pit (see page 13) with a grill grate over the coals.

Meanwhile, in a large saucepan on the stovetop, combine the potatoes and salt with enough water to cover by 2 inches (5 cm). Place the pan over high heat and bring the water to a boil. Reduce the heat and simmer until the potatoes are just tender, 10 to 15 minutes.

In a small saucepan over medium heat, melt the butter. Stir in the garlic. Cook for 2 to 3 minutes, until the garlic is fragrant but not browned. Remove from the heat. Set aside until ready to use.

Drain the potatoes and let cool slightly. Halve the potatoes lengthwise and place them in a large bowl. Generously drizzle with olive oil, season with a few pinches of salt and pepper, and toss to coat.

Arrange the potatoes, cut-side down, on the grate. Grill for 2 to 3 minutes, until charred. Flip the potatoes and grill until the skin is crisp, 2 minutes more.

Transfer to a large bowl and toss with the garlic butter, Parmesan, and parsley until coated.

BEEF AND CHORIZO BUNLESS BURGER STACKS

Whether you call them "protein-style" or bunless burgers, these vegetable-laden stacks are so boldly flavored and filling you won't miss the bun at all. And they utilize one of my favorite burger tricks—incorporating the cheese into the meat. I've often found the conventional way of melting cheese on top of the patty makes it goopy and dry before I can take my first bite. Here, I grate the pepper Jack right into the meat because it's robust enough to stand up to the spicy chorizo, and it bastes the burger as it grills, making the meat extra rich and juicy.

MAKES 4 SERVINGS

1¼ pounds (567.5 g) ground chuck

8 ounces (225 g) Mexican chorizo, casing removed

1½ teaspoons kosher salt, plus more for seasoning

¾ teaspoon black pepper, plus more for seasoning

1 cup (115 g) grated pepper Jack cheese

1 globe eggplant, cut into ½-inch (1 cm) slices

Olive oil cooking spray, for preparing the eggplant

8 to 12 butter lettuce leaves

2 beefsteak tomatoes, cut into ½-inch (1 cm) slices

1 avocado, cut into ¼-inch (0.6 cm) slices

Prepare a medium-hot two-zone fire in a fire pit (see page 13) with a grill grate over the coals.

In a large bowl, lightly mix together the ground chuck, chorizo, salt, and pepper with your clean hands until combined but still fluffy in texture. Mix in the cheese until evenly distributed. Divide the beef mixture into 4 equal portions and roll each portion into a ball. Gently pat each ball into a patty about ¾ inch (2 cm) thick and press down in the center of the patty with your thumb to make a large dimple.

Lightly mist the eggplant with cooking spray and season it with salt and pepper.

Arrange the eggplant on the grate over direct heat. Grill for about 3 minutes per side, until softened and lightly charred. Transfer the eggplant to a sheet pan.

Arrange the beef patties on the grate over direct heat. Grill undisturbed for 4 minutes. Flip the patties and grill for about 4 minutes more, until an instant-read thermometer inserted into the center of the meat registers 160°F (71°C).

Assemble each burger by layering 2 or 3 lettuce leaves on the bottom, followed by an eggplant slice, 1 tomato slice, 2 avocado slices, another eggplant slice, 1 beef patty, another tomato slice, another eggplant slice, and 2 avocado slices on top. Secure the stack with a long toothpick and serve.

SECRETS TO A JUICY BURGER

Biting into a juicy burger that melts in your mouth is one of life's great pleasures. But if you often find your patties tough and dry, these six secrets might just fix that problem.

1. **Don't go lean.** The key to any good burger is using freshly ground beef chuck with 20 to 30 percent fat for a moist, tender burger; too lean and the meat has a tendency to dry out on the grill. If you don't have a butcher available to grind the chuck for you, you can grind it at home in a stand mixer with a food grinder attachment. Or, use a food processor, being careful not to overmix the meat (which will also make it tough).

2. **Speaking of overmixing . . .** Burger meat only needs a few turns with your hands to mix in the seasonings. You're not kneading dough here! Once the meat is well seasoned, divide it into equal portions and gently pat the meat into thick disks.

3. **Don't be afraid to try burger blends.** Ground chuck is my go-to for burger meat, but you can also mix it with other (fattier) meats for added flavor and juiciness, such as ground pork, Italian sausage, fresh chorizo, or even bacon.

4. **Fat can also come from butter.** For extra richness, try adding a pat of butter inside each patty as you shape it. The butter will baste the meat from the inside out as it grills, resulting in a moist and flavorful burger.

5. **Resist the urge to flatten it.** Put down that spatula! While it might be tempting—and even seem natural—to flatten the burger as it cooks, doing so only guarantees you'll press all those delicious juices out of the meat and into the flames. If you're trying to achieve a nice, level burger patty for your toppings, try this trick instead: Make a large, shallow dimple in the middle of the patty with your thumb after you shape it. Ordinarily, when meat hits the grill, the edges of the patty heat up and cook more quickly than the middle, resulting in a puffy center. The dimple works to counteract this effect, so the middle rises to form a burger that's flat and even in thickness.

6. **Griddle—don't grill—your burgers.** If you have a tendency to overcook your burgers, grill it on a plancha or in a cast iron skillet instead. Cooking the burger in its own fat renders the beef even more tender and flavorful, as opposed to cooking it directly on the grill, which can result in your burger being overly charred (or worse, with an undercooked center).

ITALIAN BURGERS WITH BASIL MUSTARD AND GIARDINIERA

A medley of Italian ingredients makes this a standout burger for your next backyard gathering. Just as with the Beef and Chorizo Bunless Burger Stacks (page 83), this recipe incorporates the cheese into the meat—this time by pressing it between two thin patties, which keeps the whole thing creamy and moist. Though the meat is usually the star of any burger, the topping is what makes this one truly special.

MAKES 4 SERVINGS

1½ cups (336 g) Homemade Giardiniera (page 88), plus more for serving

3 tablespoons (45 g) Dijon mustard

1½ tablespoons (21 g) mayonnaise

3 tablespoons (7.5 g) thinly sliced fresh basil

1 pound (454 g) ground chuck

12 ounces (340 g) bulk hot Italian sausage

¾ teaspoon kosher salt

¼ teaspoon ground black pepper

4 slices provolone cheese

4 ciabatta rolls, split

At least 3 days before you plan to serve the burgers, make the giardiniera (page 88).

Prepare a medium-hot two-zone fire in a fire pit (see page 13) with a grill grate over the coals.

Finely chop the giardiniera. Set aside until needed.

In a small bowl, stir together the mustard, mayonnaise, and basil. Set aside.

In a large bowl, combine the ground chuck, Italian sausage, salt, and pepper. With clean hands, lightly mix the ingredients until just combined. Divide the mixture into 8 equal portions. Roll each portion into a ball and gently pat each ball into a patty about ½ inch (1 cm) thick. Sandwich 1 slice of provolone between 2 patties. Crimp the edges with your fingers to encase the cheese. Press your thumb into the center of each patty to make a large dimple.

Arrange the patties on the grate over direct heat. Grill, undisturbed, for 4 minutes. Flip the patties and grill for 3 to 4 minutes more, until an instant-read thermometer inserted into the center of the meat reaches 160°F (71°C).

Arrange the ciabatta, cut-side down, on the grate over direct heat. Grill until lightly browned and crisp, 30 seconds to 1 minute. Transfer the bottom buns to a sheet pan. Turn the top buns over and grill for 30 seconds to 1 minute, until toasted.

To assemble the burgers, slather a layer of basil mustard on the bottom half of each ciabatta bun. Add a patty and a few spoonfuls of giardiniera, and place the other half of the bun on top. Serve with more giardiniera on the side.

HOMEMADE GIARDINIERA

Giardiniera *is the Italian word for "from the garden," and the beauty of this pickled condiment is you can make it with whatever fresh vegetables (from your garden or otherwise) are at their peak. For my giardiniera, I like to use a rainbow of spring and summer vegetables such as baby squash, cauliflower, carrots, bell peppers, and cherry bomb peppers (which are mild like jalapeños). You can't really go wrong here, though you should try to avoid vegetables that can discolor the pickles (like red beets).*

I like to use organic canola oil because it's flavorless and doesn't detract from the crisp tanginess of the pickles. It also won't solidify in the fridge, but you can use any neutral or mild-flavored oil in its place, such as sunflower or avocado oil, and let the giardiniera come to room temperature before serving.

MAKES 1 QUART (ABOUT 900 G)

3 cups (weight varies) chopped or sliced mixed vegetables

1 serrano pepper, thinly sliced

¼ cup (75 g) kosher salt

2 teaspoons minced fresh oregano

½ teaspoon peppercorns, cracked

1 garlic clove, thinly sliced

¾ cup (180 ml) canola oil

¾ cup (180 ml) distilled white vinegar

In a large bowl, combine the mixed vegetables and serrano. Sprinkle the salt over the vegetables, toss to combine, and cover with water by at least 1 inch (2.5 cm). Let the vegetables sit at room temperature for at least 6 hours, or overnight. Drain the vegetables and rinse thoroughly to remove excess salt.

In a quart-size (960 ml) jar with a lid, combine the oregano, cracked peppercorns, and garlic. Add the canola oil and vinegar. Seal the jar and shake well until blended.

Pack the vegetables into the jar. With the back of a spoon, tamp down to submerge them in the brine. Re-cover the jar and refrigerate the giardiniera for 2 to 3 days before serving. (It only gets better as it ages!) Giardiniera will keep, refrigerated, for up to 3 months.

WHOLE GRILLED TROUT WITH BLOOD ORANGE AND FENNEL

Grilling an entire fish—head and all—may seem intimidating, but it's actually much more forgiving than trying to wrangle a delicate fillet on the grate. The high heat of a grill develops a deep brown crust on the skin, which helps the fish release easily from the grate. Trout, in particular, cooks quickly on the grill, and you can almost be assured that by the time the fish forms a crust on both sides, it's done. The flesh stays tender and moist, and the orange and fennel infuse it with a mildly sweet aroma that doesn't overwhelm the final dish.

MAKES 4 SERVINGS

4 blood oranges, thinly sliced

4 (14-ounce, or 395 g) whole trout, butterflied and deboned

Kosher salt

Ground black pepper

1 bunch fresh thyme

½ fennel bulb, quartered, cored, thinly sliced, fronds reserved

Olive oil cooking spray, for preparing the trout

Prepare a medium-hot single-level fire in a fire pit or charcoal grill (see page 13) with a grill grate over the coals.

Cut half the orange slices into half-moons and reserve the orange rounds for topping the trout.

Pat the trout dry with paper towels and season them inside and out with salt and pepper. Stuff each trout with 2 thyme sprigs, one-fourth of the fennel slices, and one-fourth of the orange half-moons. Layer 2 thyme sprigs and 3 orange rounds on top. Tie a long length of kitchen twine around each trout to secure the fixings. Lightly mist both sides with cooking spray.

Arrange the trout, orange-side up, on the grate over direct heat. Grill for about 5 minutes, until the flesh releases easily when you roll it over with a spatula. Flip and grill for about 5 minutes more, until the trout releases easily on the other side.

Garnish with a few fennel fronds before serving.

SEARED RIB-EYE STEAKS WITH HERBED BOARD SAUCE

Of all the cuts of steak out there, rib eyes are among my favorite for their beautiful marbling and rich flavor. Slicing through buttery ribbons of fat on a rib eye just off the grill is almost as good as taking that first bite! And those buttery juices are the key to the simple herbed sauce, which you whip together on the same cutting board that you slice the steaks.

Essentially amped-up pan drippings, the fresh and earthy "board sauce" adds a depth of flavor to the steaks without overpowering them. You can use any mixture of herbs; try oregano, rosemary, basil, mint, or tarragon, depending on what you're serving on the side.

MAKES 4 SERVINGS

FOR THE SAUCE

1 shallot, sliced

½ cup (30 g) packed fresh parsley

2 tablespoons (6 g) snipped fresh chives

4 thyme sprigs, leaves stripped

2 garlic cloves, sliced

Kosher salt

Ground black pepper

Olive oil, for drizzling

FOR THE STEAKS

2 (1-pound, or 454 g, 1- to 1½-inch-, or 2 to 3.5 cm, thick) rib-eye steaks

Kosher salt

Ground black pepper

Prepare a hot two-zone fire in a fire pit (see page 13) with a grill grate over the coals.

To make the sauce: In the center of a large cutting board, mound the shallot, parsley, chives, thyme leaves, and garlic. Finely chop them together, using your knife to scrape and combine to meld the flavors. Sprinkle with a generous pinch of salt and pepper. Drizzle with olive oil and stir the pile of aromatics and herbs with the tip of your knife. Set aside until needed.

To make the steaks: Generously season the steaks on both sides with salt and pepper. Arrange the steaks over direct heat. Grill, undisturbed, for 4 to 5 minutes. Keep an eye on the steaks, as the fat dripping off may cause flare-ups. Be prepared to move them to the cooler side of the grill if needed. Once the flames die down, move the steaks back over direct heat to finish cooking.

Flip the steaks and grill for 4 to 5 minutes more, until an instant-read thermometer inserted into the thickest part of the meat reaches 125°F (52°C) for medium-rare.

To finish the sauce: Transfer the steaks to the cutting board and place them on top of the aromatics and herbs. Let rest for 5 minutes to let the heat intensify the flavors. Slice the steak against the grain. Using tongs, toss the steaks with the herbed sauce. Divide into equal portions and serve.

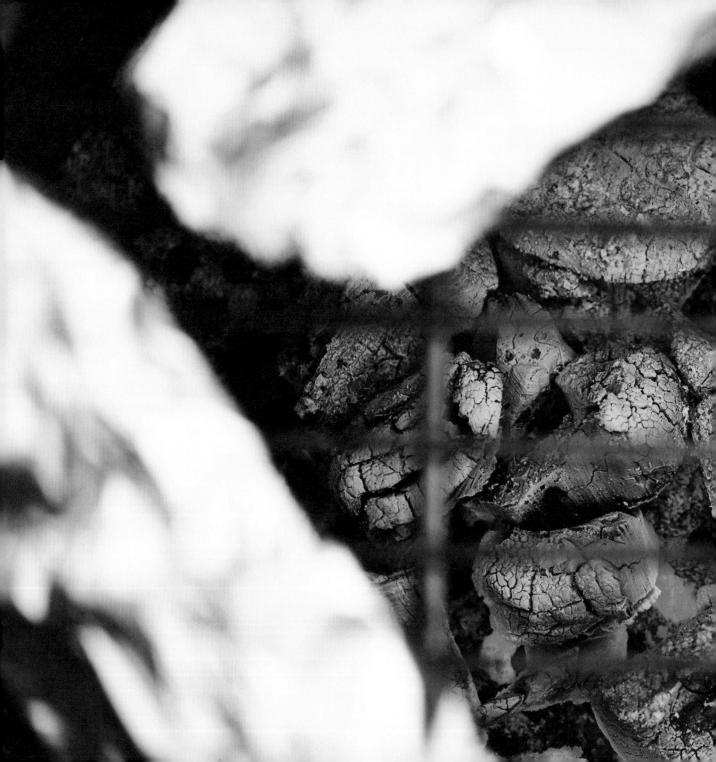

CHAPTER 4

FEASTING ... WITH FOIL PACKS

Foil packets have gone beyond the humble hobo packs of Boy Scout fame. Often lumped together with leftovers and relegated to camping food, they are so much more than appearances let on. They're mini ovens, steamers, serving bowls, and, yes, even a good way to get out of doing dishes. Crumple them up and you're done!

Despite the primitive package, there's an element of drama to cooking in a foil pack: You pile in the food, wrap it all up, put it on the fire, and hope for the best. You hear it spit and sizzle, but you won't know how it turns out until you peel it apart. The steam billows out, the smells fill your nose, and tucked inside the foil is an elegant self-contained meal— just add a fork.

FOIL PACK 101

Foil packs are nearly foolproof in their simplicity, and the learning curve is as short as these three little tips.

Oil it: A thin layer of oil keeps food from sticking to the foil. I always start with a fine mist on the surface I'm working on, even if my ingredients are well sauced or well buttered. And contrary to what you may have heard, neither side of the foil (shiny or dull) makes a difference in how heat reflective or heatproof it is.

Grill it: You can certainly set your foil packs right on the coals, but I prefer using a grill grate so I have more control over temperature. I can dial down or turn up the heat as little or as much as I need, and I don't have to worry about losing my food to the fire if I accidentally put a hole in the foil.

Rotate it: With varying levels of heat coming at it from every which way, a foil pack is bound to cook unevenly if it sits in one spot. Rotate your packs every few minutes, and even shuffle them around the grill to account for hot spots and cool spots.

Perfecting the Foil Pack

The perfect foil pack begins with a roll of heavy-duty aluminum foil and a can of olive oil cooking spray.

Step 1: Measure a large sheet of foil and lightly mist the surface with cooking spray.

Step 2: Mound the food in the center of the foil. If the ingredients are especially runny, fold the edges up slightly to form a small lip to contain the liquid.

Step 3: Bring the two longer sides together and fold the edges over twice.

Step 4: Fold each short end over twice to seal the foil packet, leaving room inside for steam to circulate.

Use a pair of tongs or a spatula to maneuver your foil packs around the grill. Always be careful when opening, as the foil pack will be full of hot steam.

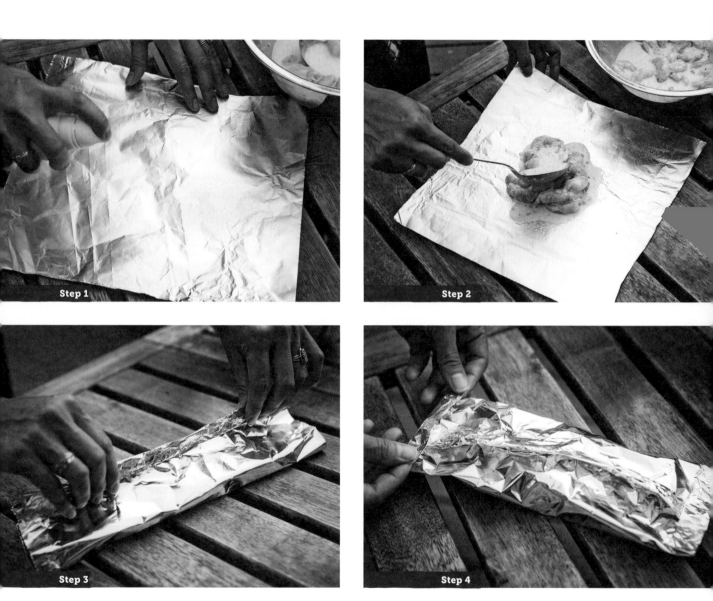

Step 1

Step 2

Step 3

Step 4

GRILL-ROASTED ELEPHANT GARLIC

Roasted elephant garlic is one of those things I like to keep around the kitchen for its endless uses. I smash and spread it on bruschetta, blend it into homemade vinaigrettes, and top my pasta, pizzas, and salads with whole cloves; mix it into mashed potatoes, whipped cauliflower, scrambled eggs, or softened butter; and sometimes just eat it straight out of the fridge with cheese and crackers. Unlike roasted garlic, which is more pungent, roasted elephant garlic is mild and sweet, making it suitable for a wider range of dishes.

MAKES 1 ROASTED GARLIC BULB

Olive oil cooking spray, for preparing the aluminum foil

1 elephant garlic bulb

1 tablespoon (15 ml) olive oil

Kosher salt

Prepare a medium-hot two-zone fire in a charcoal grill (see page 13) with a grill grate over the coals.

Measure one sheet of heavy-duty aluminum foil (at least 6 inches, or 15 cm, long) and lightly spritz the surface with cooking spray.

Holding the garlic bulb, pull the paper wrappers apart slightly at the top to expose the unpeeled cloves. Drizzle in the olive oil, making sure the oil coats most of the cloves inside. Sprinkle a generous pinch of salt into the opening and pinch the paper wrappers closed.

Center the garlic upright on the foil. Fold and seal the foil into a packet (see page 94).

Place the packet on the grate over indirect heat and close the grill lid. Roast for 45 minutes to 1 hour, until the cloves are very soft.

Transfer the foil packet to a sheet pan and let cool. Peel the cloves (or squeeze them to extract the garlic from the skins) and refrigerate the roasted garlic in an airtight container for up to 1 week. Alternatively, separate the cloves and freeze them (in their skins) in a resealable plastic freezer bag for up to 6 months.

HOT TIP

You can also bury your elephant garlic packet in the embers of a low fire when you've finished grilling for the evening. Remove the packet once the fire dies out. This is also a highly efficient way to make a big batch of roasted elephant garlic for the week, as you can piggyback on other fires and utilize them to the very end, whether you've made them in a grill, a fire pit, a campfire, or even your fireplace or woodstove.

BY THE WAY, IT'S NOT REALLY GARLIC

We call it garlic and it looks like garlic, but, in fact, elephant garlic is not a true garlic at all—it belongs to the same species as leeks (*Allium ampeloprasum*). It has a mild onion flavor that's perfect for roasting or eating raw, but the lack of pungency also means it disappears when used in soups and sauces.

SWEET POTATOES WITH SRIRACHA-MAPLE GLAZE

Sweet potatoes and maple syrup are no strangers, but this recipe marries the predictable pairing with sriracha for a balanced blend of sweet and spicy in every bite. The silky sweet potatoes have a tendency to soak up all the glaze the longer they sit, so I recommend tossing them with the sriracha and maple syrup right before serving for the brightest punch of flavor.

MAKES 4 SERVINGS

Olive oil cooking spray, for preparing the aluminum foil

3 sweet potatoes (about 1½ pounds, or 681 g), cut into 1-inch (2.5 cm) chunks

Kosher salt

2 tablespoons (28 g) butter, cut into small pats

2 tablespoons (30 ml) maple syrup

2 teaspoons sriracha

⅓ cup (37 g) chopped walnuts

HOT TIP

There's no need to peel sweet potatoes! The skins are edible, are full of nutrients, and add subtle texture. Simply scrub them with a vegetable brush under running water to make sure they're clean before cooking.

Prepare a medium-hot single-level fire in a charcoal grill or fire pit (see page 13) with a grill grate over the coals.

Measure two sheets of heavy-duty aluminum foil (at least 16 inches, or 40 cm, long) and lightly spray the surface with cooking spray.

Divide the sweet potatoes between the two prepared sheets, piling them in the center. Mist the sweet potatoes with cooking spray, season with salt, and scatter the butter over the top. Fold and seal the foil into packets (see page 94).

Place the packets on the grate. Grill for 20 to 25 minutes, until the sweet potatoes are tender, rotating the packets every 5 to 10 minutes for even cooking.

Meanwhile, in a small bowl, stir together the maple syrup and sriracha until combined.

Transfer the foil packets to a sheet pan and use caution when opening, as they will be full of steam. Drizzle the maple syrup mixture over the sweet potatoes, sprinkle with the walnuts, and gently toss to coat.

WILD MUSHROOMS WITH SOY-SCALLION BUTTER

If you love deep umami flavor, the unlikely yet delicious combination of soy sauce and butter is one you'll be reaching for over and over. It's simple and comforting, warm and luxurious, and can turn an ordinary meal into an elegant dish—try it on rice, noodles, even popcorn! Mushrooms, in particular, soak up the sauce exceptionally well while keeping their meaty, velvety texture. Try a variety of cultivated wild mushrooms in this recipe, such as oyster, shiitake, king trumpet, and brown and white beech mushrooms.

MAKES 4 SERVINGS

Olive oil cooking spray, for preparing the aluminum foil

8 tablespoons (1 stick, or 112 g) butter, at room temperature

2 tablespoons (30 ml) soy sauce

½ cup (50 g) minced scallion, white and green parts, plus more for garnishing, divided

1 pound (454 g) mixed wild mushrooms, sliced or torn into ¼- to ½-inch (0.6 to 1 cm) pieces

3 tablespoons (45 ml) olive oil

Kosher salt

Ground black pepper

Prepare a hot single-level fire in a fire pit or charcoal grill (see page 26) with a grill grate over the coals.

Measure two sheets of heavy-duty aluminum foil (at least 14 inches, or 35 cm, long) and lightly spritz the surface with cooking spray.

In a small bowl, using a fork, mash the butter and soy sauce until well combined. Stir in half the scallions.

In a large bowl, drizzle the mushrooms with the olive oil and season with salt and pepper. Add the remaining scallions and toss to coat.

Divide the mushroom mixture between the prepared foil sheets, piling them in the center. Dot with the soy-scallion butter. Fold and seal the foil into packets (see page 94).

Place the foil packets on the grate. Grill for about 15 minutes, rotating every 5 minutes for even cooking. Transfer the foil packets to a sheet pan and use caution when opening, as they will be full of steam.

Garnish with a sprinkle of scallions before serving.

POTATO AND PROSCIUTTO PACKETS

Whether you're looking for a simple side dish to serve with your main course or a potluck item you can take to a tailgate, foil-packet potatoes are always a crowd-pleaser. They're quick to throw together and tough to mess up, as long as you give them enough time on the grill to turn fluffy and velvety. In this recipe, Yukon gold potatoes get gussied up with creamy goat cheese and salty prosciutto, a sublime combination that goes well with almost any dish.

MAKES 4 SERVINGS

2 pounds (908 g) Yukon gold potatoes, cut into ¼-inch (0.6 cm) slices

1 tablespoon (15 ml) olive oil

1 tablespoon (2 g) minced fresh rosemary

Kosher salt

Ground black pepper

Olive oil cooking spray, for preparing the aluminum foil

4 thin slices prosciutto

4 ounces (115 g) goat cheese

Prepare a hot single-level fire in a fire pit or charcoal grill (see page 13) with a grill grate over the coals.

In a large bowl, toss the potatoes with the olive oil, rosemary, and a few pinches of salt and pepper to evenly coat.

Measure four sheets of heavy-duty aluminum foil (at least 14 inches, or 35 cm, long) and spritz the surface of each sheet with cooking spray.

Mound an equal portion of potatoes in the center of each prepared foil sheet. Drape 1 slice of prosciutto over each mound. Top each with a few dollops of goat cheese and fold and seal the foil into packets (see page 94).

Place the packets on the grate. Grill for about 35 minutes, rotating every 10 minutes for even cooking. Transfer the foil packets to a sheet pan and use caution when opening, as they will be full of steam. The potatoes are done when the flesh is easily pierced with a fork.

FOIL PACK FRENCH DIP

Great for camping or casual meals at home, this nontraditional French dip is a fun pull-apart sandwich that comes together quickly, thanks to a couple of shortcuts: roast beef from the deli and a quick "au jus" made from butter. We might not have a homemade roast or a pan full of drippings, but we definitely aren't short on flavor here. Keep in mind the au jus will only be as good as your beef broth, so it's worth using a well-seasoned homemade broth or seeking out quality bone broth from a butcher shop.

MAKES 6 SERVINGS

Olive oil cooking spray, for preparing the aluminum foil

FOR THE AU JUS

4 tablespoons (½ stick, or 56 g) butter

1 tablespoon (8 g) all-purpose flour

2 cups (480 ml) well-seasoned beef broth

½ teaspoon Worcestershire sauce

Kosher salt

Ground black pepper

FOR THE SANDWICHES

8 tablespoons (1 stick, or 112 g) butter, at room temperature

1 tablespoon (4 g) minced fresh parsley

1 teaspoon Worcestershire sauce

1 teaspoon garlic powder

1 teaspoon onion powder

½ teaspoon ground black pepper

1 (1-pound, or 454 g) loaf French bread (about 16 inches, or 40 cm, long), halved widthwise so you have 2 (8-inch, or 20 cm) loaves

Dijon mustard, for spreading

12 slices provolone cheese

1 pound (454 g) thinly sliced deli roast beef

RECIPE CONTINUES

Prepare a medium-hot two-zone fire in a charcoal grill (see page 13) with a grill grate over the coals.

Measure two sheets of heavy-duty aluminum foil (at least 18 inches, or 45 cm, long) and mist the surface of each sheet with cooking spray. Set aside until needed.

To make the au jus: On the stovetop, in a medium saucepan over medium heat, melt the butter. Whisk the flour into the butter and cook, whisking frequently, until the flour is incorporated and the mixture thickens, 2 to 3 minutes.

Add the broth and Worcestershire and whisk to combine. Increase the heat and bring the mixture to a boil. Boil the au jus until it thickens slightly. Season to taste with salt and pepper. Keep warm until ready to use.

To make the sandwiches: In a small bowl, using a fork, mash the butter, parsley, Worcestershire, garlic powder, onion powder, and pepper until well combined.

Cut even slits about ½ inch (1 cm) apart in each loaf, stopping just before you slice through the bottom so the slices hold together. You should have 12 equal "slices" of bread per loaf.

Spread a thin layer of the butter mixture on one side of every other slice. Spread a thin layer of Dijon on the opposite side of each buttered slice. Starting at the end of each loaf, tuck 1 slice of provolone and 2 slices of roast beef between the buttered and Dijon sides, so when the bread is pulled apart when serving they will become individual sandwiches.

Place a loaf in the center of each prepared foil sheet and lightly coat the tops and sides of the bread with the remaining butter mixture. Fold and seal the foil into packets (see page 94).

Place the foil packets on the grate over direct heat. Grill for 5 to 10 minutes, turning frequently, until the bread is toasted and the cheese is melted. If you'd like to add a bit more crispness, move the foil packs over indirect heat, open the packs to expose the top and sides of each loaf, and close the grill lid. Continue grilling for about 5 minutes more, until the bread is golden brown all the way through.

Serve the French dips family style with au jus on the side and let your guests pull apart their own sandwiches.

GARLICKY SALMON

Garlic lovers, this recipe is for you! And it's so easy to pull off you can pick up a salmon on your way home and prepare it in a few minutes with a handful of pantry staples. I love serving a large platter of salmon like this alongside grilled vegetables for a well-rounded meal that requires little hands-on time and even fewer dishes to do. It's a weeknight win all around!

MAKES 4 SERVINGS

2 tablespoons (28 g) butter

6 garlic cloves, chopped

2 tablespoons (30 ml) dry white wine

1 tablespoon (15 ml) fresh lemon juice

Olive oil cooking spray, for preparing the aluminum foil

1 (1½- to 2-pound, or 681 to 908 g) side of salmon

Kosher salt

Ground black pepper

1 lemon, halved crosswise

Finely chopped fresh parsley, for garnishing

Prepare a medium-hot single-level fire in a fire pit or charcoal grill (see page 13) with a grill grate over the coals.

On the stovetop, in a small saucepan over medium heat, melt the butter. Add the garlic. Cook until fragrant, 1 to 2 minutes. Stir in the white wine and lemon juice. Bring the sauce to a simmer, cook for 1 minute, and remove from the heat.

Measure a sheet of heavy-duty aluminum foil (at least 18 inches, or 45 cm, long, or long enough to wrap the salmon) and lightly spritz the surface with cooking spray.

Pat the salmon dry with paper towels and place it in the center of the prepared foil sheet. Pour the sauce evenly over the top and season with salt and pepper. Fold and seal the foil into a packet (see page 94).

Place the packet on the grate. Grill for 10 to 12 minutes, rotating the packet every 3 to 5 minutes for even cooking. (Depending on the thickness of your salmon, cooking time may vary by a few minutes.) Transfer the foil packet to a sheet pan and use caution when opening, as it will be full of steam. The salmon is done when the flesh flakes easily with a fork and an instant-read thermometer inserted into the thickest part of the flesh registers 120°F to 125°F (49°C to 52°C).

Lightly mist the lemon halves with cooking spray and place them, cut-side down, on the grate. Grill for about 5 minutes, until the edges are charred. Squeeze the lemons over the salmon and garnish with a sprinkle of parsley. Serve the salmon family style or cut it into individual portions for plating.

MAKING THE CUT

This book uses a variety of salmon on the grill, including salmon fillets (page 216) and salmon steaks (page 153). But what are the differences between these cuts?

Side of salmon: This impressive cut is a single, large fillet that runs the length of the fish and has been cleaned and deboned. A whole side of salmon averages 4 to 5 pounds (1.8 to 2.3 kg), feeding eight to ten people, but can be cut into smaller sections. It's best for grilling in foil or grill-roasting on a plank, because the delicate flesh and large size make it hard to turn over. A side of salmon can be served family style or cut into individual fillets for plating.

Salmon fillet: When you slice a whole side of salmon into 6- to 8-ounce (170 to 225 g) portions, you get fillets. Most fillets are cut from the tail end of the fish, and the tapering thickness often leads to overcooking the thinner piece of flesh. To remedy this, ask your fishmonger to give you center-cut fillets, which have an even thickness. If you're cooking for four people, ask the fishmonger to cut a whole side of salmon in half and give you the thicker half. You'll end up with about a 2-pound (908 g) fillet you can cut into smaller fillets at home. They can be grilled with the skin on, grilled in foil, or grilled on a plank or plancha.

Salmon steak: This uniformly thick piece of salmon is cut perpendicular to the spine, resulting in a U-shaped cross-section that includes the skin and bones. Each hefty 8- to 10-ounce (225 to 280 g) steak truly feels like a steak with its meaty texture, making it ideal for searing on a plancha or in a cast iron skillet. Salmon steaks can sometimes be hard to find at the fish counter, so it's best to call ahead or special order what you need. For most recipes that call for salmon steaks, fillets can be used in their place with an adjustment in cooking time. A general rule is to allow 5 minutes of cooking time for each ½ inch (1 cm) of thickness.

SHRIMP IN SPICY COCONUT SAUCE

With lemongrass, ginger, zesty lime, and spicy sambal oelek mingling in an umami-boosted coconut broth, it's almost hard to believe this silky, fragrant sauce came together in mere minutes! Toss in some tender shrimp, which easily soak up the pungent flavors, and you have a weeknight meal that hits all the right notes on the taste buds.

YIELD: SERVES 4

Olive oil cooking spray, for preparing the aluminum foil

½ cup (120 ml) coconut milk

¼ cup (60 ml) fresh lime juice

1 tablespoon (15 ml) fish sauce

2 teaspoons sambal oelek (Asian chile paste)

1 tablespoon (9 g) minced lemongrass, tender interior only

1 tablespoon (6 g) minced peeled fresh ginger

1½ pounds (681 g) large shrimp, peeled and deveined

Steamed jasmine rice, for serving

Prepare a medium-hot single-level fire in a fire pit or charcoal grill (see page 13) with a grill grate over the coals.

Measure four sheets of heavy-duty aluminum foil (at least 14 inches, or 35 cm, long) and lightly spray the surface of each sheet with cooking spray.

In a large bowl, stir together the coconut milk, lime juice, fish sauce, sambal oelek, lemongrass, and ginger. Add the shrimp and toss to coat.

Mound an equal portion of the shrimp in the center of each prepared foil sheet. Fold all four sides up on each sheet (as if you were making a bowl) and divide any remaining coconut sauce among the packets. Fold and seal the foil into packets (see page 94).

Place the foil packets on the grate. Grill for 5 to 10 minutes, rotating every 2 minutes for even cooking. Transfer the packets to a sheet pan and use caution when opening, as they will be full of steam. The shrimp are done when the flesh is opaque. Serve the shrimp over bowls of steamed jasmine rice.

SPICY SMOKED SAUSAGE, SNAP BEANS, AND POTATOES

When I make foil packets, it's usually to save time and have an easy side dish ready while the main event is on the grill. But this recipe is so flavorful and filling on its own it can be the main event! I like to make a few of these packets to bring camping or tailgating, too—they hold well and travel well, and my favorite Cajun Creole spice blend (an intermingling of fiery, savory, and earthy flavors) keeps them from being boring.

MAKES 4 SERVINGS

1 pound (454 g) smoked andouille sausage, cut into ½-inch (1 cm) slices

1 pound (454 g) baby potatoes, quartered

8 ounces (225 g) snap beans, trimmed and halved

8 ounces (225 g) cremini mushrooms, quartered

1 yellow onion, chopped

2 tablespoons (30 ml) olive oil

4 teaspoons (10 g) Cajun Creole Spice Blend (recipe follows)

Olive oil cooking spray, for preparing the aluminum foil

4 tablespoons (½ stick, or 56 g) butter, cut into small pats

Handful chopped fresh parsley, for garnishing

Prepare a hot single-level fire in a fire pit or charcoal grill (see page 13) with a grill grate over the coals.

In a large bowl, combine the sausage, potatoes, snap beans, mushrooms, and onion. Drizzle with the olive oil and sprinkle the spice blend over. Toss to coat.

Measure four sheets of heavy-duty aluminum foil (at least 14 inches, or 35 cm, long) and mist the surface of each sheet with cooking spray.

Evenly divide the sausage-vegetable mixture among the prepared foil sheets, heaping them into a mound in the center. Scatter a few pats of butter over each mound and fold and seal the foil into packets (see page 94).

Place the packets on the grate. Grill for about 35 minutes, rotating the packets every 10 minutes for even cooking. Transfer the foil packets to a sheet pan and use caution when opening, as they will be full of steam. The vegetables are done when the potatoes are easily pierced with a fork.

Garnish each packet with a sprinkle of parsley before serving.

> **HOT TIP**
>
> To ensure the potatoes cook all the way through, halve or quarter them into chunks no larger than ½ inch (1 cm).

CAJUN CREOLE SPICE BLEND

Inspired by the mosaic of French, Spanish, African, and Caribbean cultures that flourishes in New Orleans, this seasoning blend imparts a robust smoky flavor, mild kick, and deep color to dishes. It's also featured in my Juicy Jumbo Creole Shrimp (page 137) and Dutch Oven Jambalaya (page 128).

MAKES ½ CUP (60 G)

2 tablespoons (17 g) paprika

1 tablespoon (18 g) kosher salt

1 tablespoon (9 g) garlic powder

1 tablespoon (7 g) onion powder

2 teaspoons dried oregano

2 teaspoons dried basil

2 teaspoons dried thyme

1 teaspoon cayenne pepper

1 teaspoon ground black pepper

1 teaspoon ground white pepper

In a small bowl, stir together all the ingredients. Transfer the spice blend to an airtight lidded container and store in a cool, dark, dry place until needed. The spice blend will keep for up to 6 months, after which it will start to lose potency.

GARLIC BUTTER GNOCCHI AND MUSHROOMS

This hearty recipe is simple enough to prepare and stow for a weeknight meal, yet full of flavor and texture thanks to the plump, velvety gnocchi, the silky umami-rich mushrooms, and the garlicky, buttery broth they steam in. I like to use packaged Parmesan gnocchi for an added layer of flavor, but there's no reason you couldn't finish this dish with a sprinkle of freshly grated Parmesan cheese. To take it up a notch, try it with a medley of wild mushrooms like chanterelle, morel, and maitake.

MAKES 4 SERVINGS

20 ounces (569 g) fresh gnocchi

12 ounces (340 g) cremini mushrooms, quartered

Olive oil, for drizzling

4 garlic cloves, minced

1 teaspoon kosher salt

½ teaspoon red pepper flakes

¼ teaspoon ground black pepper

Olive oil cooking spray, for preparing the aluminum foil

1 cup (240 ml) chicken broth, or ½ cup (120 ml) chicken broth and ½ cup (120 ml) dry white wine

4 tablespoons (½ stick, or 56 g) butter, cut into pats

Finely chopped fresh parsley, for garnishing

Prepare a hot single-level fire in a fire pit or charcoal grill (see page 13) with a grill grate over the coals.

In a large bowl, combine the gnocchi and mushrooms. Generously drizzle with olive oil. Add the garlic, salt, red pepper flakes, and black pepper and toss until coated.

Measure four sheets of heavy-duty aluminum foil (at least 14 inches, or 35 cm, long) and spritz the surface of each sheet with cooking spray.

Pile an equal portion of the gnocchi and mushroom mixture in the center of each prepared foil sheet. Fold all four sides up on each sheet (as if you were making a bowl) and pour ¼ cup (60 ml) of chicken broth into each packet. Scatter a few pats of butter over the top of each and fold and seal the foil into packets (see page 94).

Place the packets on the grate. Grill for about 15 minutes, rotating every 5 minutes for even cooking. Transfer the foil packets to a sheet pan and use caution when opening, as they will be full of steam.

GLAZED CINNAMON-SUGAR PEACHES

Add this to your list of no-fail, no-fuss desserts by the fire: It's lovely on its own, with bits of caramelized sugar and a touch of cinnamon, but even better when paired with a scoop of vanilla ice cream and, perhaps, a slice of grilled pound cake. It also holds well, so you can grill it right after your main course to take advantage of the initial heat. Come dessert time, simply reheat the peaches in their foil packets over the last of the coals.

MAKES 4 TO 8 SERVINGS

Olive oil cooking spray, for preparing the aluminum foil

4 peaches, pitted and quartered

3 tablespoons (36 g) packed light brown sugar

¼ teaspoon ground cinnamon

2 tablespoons (28 g) butter, cut into small pats

Prepare a medium-hot single-level fire in a fire pit or charcoal grill (see page 13) with a grill grate over the coals.

Measure four sheets of heavy-duty aluminum foil (at least 16 inches, or 40 cm, long) and mist the surface with cooking spray.

Divide the peaches among the foil, placing them in the center of each prepared foil sheet, and sprinkle the brown sugar and cinnamon over them. Dot the peaches with the butter and fold and seal the foil into packets (see page 94).

Place the packets on the grate. Grill for 10 to 12 minutes, rotating every 3 minutes for even cooking. Transfer the foil packets to a sheet pan and use caution when opening, as they will be full of steam.

BERRY BRIOCHE BREAD PUDDING

Confession: I originally envisioned this bread pudding as a dessert.

But, you see, an unintended hazard of being a cookbook author is having ample leftovers. This bread pudding was one of the recipes that ended up in the fridge at the end of the day, untouched. Maybe it was meant to be, because I had it for breakfast the next morning and now I can't imagine having to sit through a whole meal before I can enjoy it! The bread pudding is light and creamy, sweet but not cloying, and has a subtle fragrance from the splash of bourbon (a surprising little treat!).

You can use fresh brioche as long as you give it a minimum 30-minute soaking time in the custard, but day-old brioche will work like a sponge to become wonderfully suffused with all that flavor and texture.

MAKES 4 SERVINGS

Olive oil cooking spray, for preparing the aluminum foil

2 large eggs

½ cup (120 ml) milk

½ cup (120 ml) heavy cream

⅓ cup (67 g) sugar

1 tablespoon (15 ml) bourbon

¼ teaspoon ground cinnamon

5 (1-inch, or 2.5 cm) slices brioche bread, cut into 1-inch (2.5 cm) cubes

1 heaping cup (140 g) mixed berries

1 tablespoon (14 g) butter, cut into small pats

Prepare a medium two-zone fire in a charcoal grill (see page 13) with a grill grate over the coals.

Measure one sheet of heavy-duty aluminum foil (at least 22 inches, or 55 cm, long) and lightly spray the surface with cooking spray.

In a large bowl, whisk the eggs, milk, heavy cream, sugar, bourbon, and cinnamon until well blended. Stir in the bread cubes until coated and let soak in the custard for at least 30 minutes. Fold in the berries.

Lay the soaked bread and berries in the center of the prepared foil sheet and dot with the butter. Fold and seal the foil into a packet (see page 94).

Place the packet on the grate over indirect heat and close the grill lid. Grill for 30 to 40 minutes, rotating the packet every 10 minutes for even cooking, until the custard is set but still a little wobbly and the bread is browned around the edges.

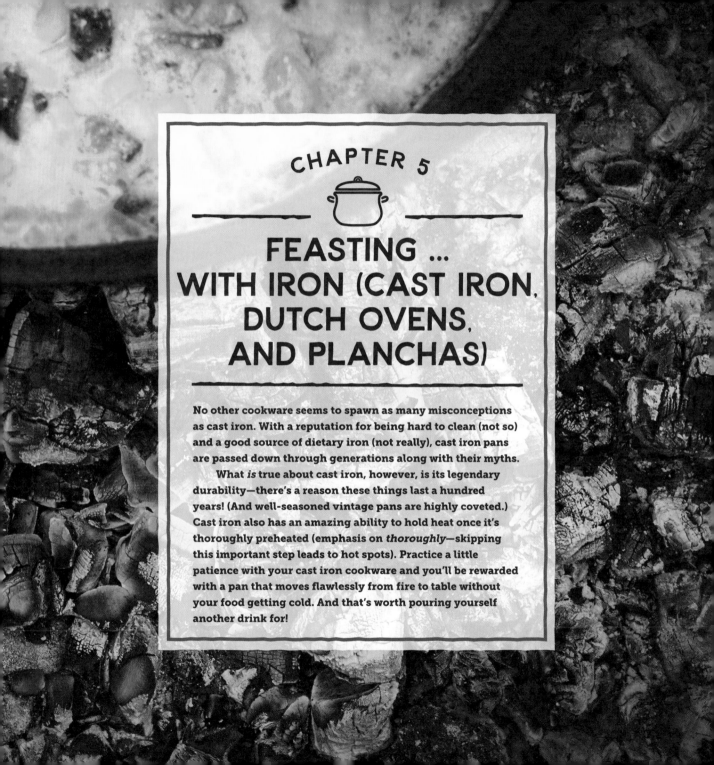

CHAPTER 5

FEASTING ... WITH IRON (CAST IRON, DUTCH OVENS, AND PLANCHAS)

No other cookware seems to spawn as many misconceptions as cast iron. With a reputation for being hard to clean (not so) and a good source of dietary iron (not really), cast iron pans are passed down through generations along with their myths.

What *is* true about cast iron, however, is its legendary durability—there's a reason these things last a hundred years! (And well-seasoned vintage pans are highly coveted.) Cast iron also has an amazing ability to hold heat once it's thoroughly preheated (emphasis on *thoroughly*—skipping this important step leads to hot spots). Practice a little patience with your cast iron cookware and you'll be rewarded with a pan that moves flawlessly from fire to table without your food getting cold. And that's worth pouring yourself another drink for!

THE BIG THREE OF CAST IRON

Inexpensive and tough as nails, these versatile workhorses allow you to make any of the cast iron recipes in this book, as well as open your fire pit or grill to countless new meals you may not have thought were possible over a fire.

12-inch (30 cm) skillet: A good all-around size, this pan can cook up a meal for four people. I highly recommend buying an ovenproof lid for it, or repurposing an ovenproof lid from another pan that fits it well.

8-quart (7.7 L) Dutch oven: Some Dutch ovens are designed for stovetop and oven use, but the one you want is the classic camping version with three feet and a flanged lid. These features allow you to place coals under and on top of the Dutch oven to heat it.

15 x 17-inch (37.5 x 43 cm) plancha: Essentially a griddle, planchas are popular in Spain and many other parts of the world, where the fiery style of cooking involves grilling food on a hot metal slab. I prefer a plancha with a shallow rim, as it helps corral the ingredients when I'm turning and tossing them.

You will also need vegetable oil for seasoning (I prefer canola oil) and a plastic pan scraper for cleaning.

Useful accessories to have for Dutch oven cooking include a lid lifter, a wire rack or other heatproof landing zone for the lid, and a whisk broom for sweeping coals and ash off the lid.

Seasoning Your Cast Iron

Modern cast iron cookware comes preseasoned from the factory, but it doesn't hurt to season again when you bring the cookware home. Rinse and dry the cookware and heat it on the stovetop until smoking. Apply a very thin layer of oil to the cast iron and rub it

HOT TIP

Seasoning is not merely a slick of oil on your cast iron cookware that makes it nonstick. Seasoning is polymerized oil—a layer of oil chemically bonded to the metal through repeated oiling and heating. This results in a plastic-like coating on the cast iron that becomes stronger over time with additional seasoning.

in thoroughly with a paper towel (across the bottom, up and down the sides, and along the handle). Buff it out with a clean towel and turn off the heat. Let the cast iron cool completely, then reheat and repeat the process several times to build up the seasoning.

Alternatively, season your cookware in the oven. Rinse, dry, oil, and buff the cast iron inside and out, and set it upside down in a cold oven. Place a large sheet of foil underneath to catch any drips. Heat the oven to 450°F (230°C). Bake for 1 hour, turn off the oven, and let the cookware cool inside. Repeat the process as many times as needed until the cast iron achieves a smooth, subtle, evenly dark sheen. If it feels sticky or looks blotchy after seasoning, it's likely you used too much oil. Simply scrub it off, wash with soap, and try again.

Properly seasoned cookware is more durable than most people think, so it's fine to use metal utensils, stainless steel scrubbers, and scouring pads on your cast iron without fear of removing the seasoning.

Cleaning and Caring for Cast Iron

There's a common misconception you should never wash your cast iron cookware, but a mild dishwashing soap is harmless to the seasoning and actually helpful for getting all the gunk off the surface (gunk such as old grease, rancid oil, and other undesirables that linger on unwashed cookware).

The important thing to remember is **never put cold water on hot cast iron**. The thermal shock could cause the cast iron to crack.

For safe and easy cleaning, wait until the cast

iron has cooled enough to handle. Scrape off any food remnants and wash your cookware with a dab of soap and a dish scrubber. You can also sprinkle a handful of kosher salt on the surface and work it in with your brush for extra scrubbing power. If any stubborn spots remain, boil some water in the cookware until the burnt-on bits soften and release. Rinse well and dry with a towel. Set the cookware on the stovetop over medium-low heat until the cast iron is completely dry. Season with a light layer of oil, wipe the excess oil with a clean towel, remove from the heat, and let cool.

Store your cast iron in a clean, dry place to discourage rust. Use it regularly to improve the seasoning and never leave it soaking in water. Avoid cooking with very acidic foods (such as citrus, wine, and tomato sauce) until the cast iron is well seasoned.

If your cookware has a few rust spots, you can soak it in a 50/50 solution of distilled white vinegar and water for at least 1 hour (up to 6 hours) until the rust dissolves. If your cookware is severely rusted, however, you can use steel wool to strip the seasoning and scrape it down to bare iron before re-seasoning in the oven.

COOKING WITH A DUTCH OVEN

Dutch ovens are made for the volatility of live-fire cooking, as they're very forgiving in less-than-ideal conditions. Used as ovens or pots, they adapt to a wide range of recipes and require no special space of their own. You can simply set a galvanized steel oil pan on a heatproof surface and spread your coals in it, or place a double layer of heavy-duty aluminum foil on dirt to start cooking.

Arranging the Coals

Longtime standards for controlling temperature in a Dutch oven involve setting specific numbers of coals below the oven and on the lid. These formulas work well when using charcoal briquettes, but with hardwood and hardwood lump charcoal—which are not consistently sized—it's difficult to go by the coal-counting method. An easier way to regulate temperature for Dutch oven cooking is to use the "ring method."

In this book, I specify temperature as 1 ring, 1½ rings, 2 rings, or a full spread.

+ **1 ring:** A circle of coals with all the coals touching. The outside edge of the circle is lined up with the outside edge of the Dutch oven, top or bottom.

+ **1½ rings:** The same as 1 ring with an additional ½ ring inside, touching the first ring. A ½ ring is a circle of coals with every other coal taken out.

+ **2 rings:** A second ring of coals is placed inside the first ring, with both rings touching.

+ **Full spread:** The coals are spread out in a single even layer with all coals touching.

Using a combination of rings for top and bottom heating allows you to reach the approximate temperature needed for baking, boiling, and browning. For baking, I always start with 1 ring on the bottom as a "burner," and then place either 1½ rings on top for medium heat (350°F to 375°F, or 180°C to 190°C) or 2 rings on top for high heat (400°F to 425°F, or 200°C to 220°C). For searing, frying, or boiling, I concentrate all the heat on the bottom with a full spread of coals.

Using a pair of tongs or a grill rake, break apart odd-shape or oversize coals into roughly the same size so they're easier to manage. Remember that different types of wood and charcoal, outside air temperature, wind, sun, and shade can all affect heat output, so trust your senses and adjust the rings as needed to work with your conditions. The best way to master temperature control on a Dutch oven is to stay loyal to the same brand of lump charcoal or the same type of wood. With practice, you'll learn how hot a ring of coals makes your oven and how much you need each time you cook.

Coals also burn out at different rates and develop hot spots. It's helpful to rotate the Dutch oven and/or lid 180 degrees every 20 minutes or so while your food cooks to encourage even heating. This is also a good time to supplement or replenish the coals to maintain temperature.

CAST-IRON CLAMBAKE

Though the beloved summer ritual of a clambake usually involves a beach and a sunset, that doesn't mean you can't have one in your backyard—even if it's many miles from the coast. I've simplified this clambake for a Dutch oven by using only clams, but if you have a bigger pot you don't mind throwing on the fire, add shrimp, fish, crab, and even lobster for a whole seafood boil.

And speaking of boil . . . this clambake is actually a clam boil. The trick to not overcooking the clams is layering the ingredients so those that need the most cooking are closest to the coals: potatoes first, then sausages, corn, and clams on top, which steam in a fragrant bath of beer and Old Bay. I like to use a summer ale for the complex fruity aromas it offers, but any light beer will work. (Or try a bottle of white wine!)

MAKES 6 SERVINGS

2 (12-ounce, or 300 ml) bottles light beer

½ cup (30 g) packed whole parsley leaves

2 tablespoons (14 g) Old Bay seasoning

2 bay leaves

2 pounds (908 g) new potatoes (about 1 inch, or 2.5 cm, in diameter)

1 pound (454 g) andouille sausage, cut diagonally into 2-inch (5 cm) slices

4 ears corn, shucked and cut into thirds

3 pounds (1.35 kg) littleneck clams, cleaned

Chopped fresh chives, for garnishing

Lemon wedges, for serving

½ cup (120 ml) melted butter

Prepare a mound of wood coals or hardwood lump charcoal (see page 12).

Move about 2 quarts' (400 g) worth of coals to the cooking pit and arrange them in a full spread (see page 120).

In a well-seasoned Dutch oven, combine the beer, parsley, Old Bay, and bay leaves. Add the potatoes in a single layer and spread the sausages on top. Fill the Dutch oven with just enough water to cover the ingredients. Place the lid on the Dutch oven, nestle it on the coals, and bring to a boil. Cook for about 15 minutes, until the potatoes are just tender.

Add the corn. Layer the clams on top. Replenish the coals, if needed, to maintain a boil. Cover and cook until the clams begin to open and the corn is tender, 10 to 12 minutes. Discard any clams that do not open.

Using a slotted spoon or skimmer, transfer the clams, sausages, and vegetables to sheet pans and garnish with a sprinkle of chives. Ladle the broth into small bowls for each guest.

Heap the food onto a newspaper-lined table or serve family style from the sheet pans with lemon wedges on the side. Offer the broth and melted butter at the table for dipping.

HOW OPEN IS OPEN?

Every recipe for live clams instructs you to cook until the clams are open—but how open is open? And what do you do with clams that start off slightly open? Here's the lowdown on how to tell when your clams are safe to cook and eat.

Buy from a reputable fishmonger. It goes without saying that you should source your seafood from a fishmonger who knows their suppliers well and has a quick turnover. A good fishmonger is also knowledgeable about all the fish and shellfish they carry, so don't be afraid to ask about differences in varieties or tips on preparing them.

Take a whiff. Once you have your clams in hand, stick your nose in the bag and take a good whiff. If the clams smell like anything other than the sea, give them back or try another fishmonger.

Do the tap test. While most clams are tightly shut when you buy them, some appear to "smile" at you—that is, their shells are slightly gaping. To determine whether they're good, simply give them a light tap on the sink. Their muscles should close the shells in defense. If they don't, toss 'em. You can also squeeze the shells together; if they spring open again, the clam is dead and must be discarded (because you don't know how long it's been dead).

Open wide? Quite the contrary. By the time you wait for the clams to open all the way, they're likely overcooked. You'll know they're done when the shells just begin to open, at which point they can be removed from the pot and your fingers can do the rest of the work. Stirring the clams for about 5 minutes after you add them to the pot helps redistribute and cook them more evenly, as clams piled together may not be able to open fully.

DRY INGREDIENTS

2 cups (248 g) all-purpose flour

¼ cup (50 g) granulated sugar

2 teaspoons baking powder

1 teaspoon baking soda

½ teaspoon kosher salt

WET INGREDIENTS

2½ cups (600 ml) buttermilk, shaken

2 large eggs, lightly beaten

4 tablespoons (60 ml) melted butter

1 teaspoon vanilla extract

OTHER PANCAKE INGREDIENTS

2 tablespoons (28 g) butter

1½ cups (190 g) fresh raspberries, plus more for serving

Confectioners' sugar, for dusting

Slivered almonds, for serving

Maple syrup, for serving

DUTCH OVEN–BAKED BUTTERMILK PANCAKE WITH RASPBERRIES AND ALMONDS

If one of your peeves with having pancakes for breakfast is sitting down to luke-warm pancakes, or eating by yourself after everyone else has already finished the pancakes you made for them, try a baked pancake. It finishes in the same amount of time it takes to make the same amount of traditional pancakes for the whole family.

While you don't get the nicely browned exterior that you do with griddled pan-cakes, what they lack in color, they more than make up for in texture and flavor. These luscious 1-inch (2.5 cm)-thick slices are soft, spongy, and airy with a tart zing in every bite from fresh raspberries.

MAKES 4 TO 8 SERVINGS

Prepare a mound of wood coals or hardwood lump charcoal (see page 12).

Move about 1 quart's worth (200 g) of coals to the cooking pit and arrange them in a ring (see page 120). Place a well-seasoned Dutch oven over the coals and preheat for 10 minutes.

In a medium bowl, combine all the dry ingredients. Lightly whisk in the wet ingredients until no dry pockets remain but the batter is still a little lumpy. Let the batter sit for at least 10 minutes while the Dutch oven preheats.

In the hot Dutch oven, melt the butter and swirl it around to coat the bottom. Pour in the pancake batter and smooth the top with a rubber spatula. Sprinkle the raspberries over the batter. Cover the Dutch oven with a lid and place 2 rings of coals on top (see page 120).

Bake for 35 to 40 minutes, until the pancake is slightly browned and crisp on the edges and a toothpick inserted in the center comes out clean.

Dust the pancake with confectioners' sugar and sprinkle with almonds and more raspberries. Cut into 8 equal slices and serve with a drizzle of maple syrup.

HOT TIP

The secret to light, fluffy pancakes is remembering not to whisk your batter into oblivion—good pancake batter should have small to medium lumps in it.

DUTCH OVEN CREAMY CORN CHOWDER

This is the type of meal I love to make when the weather's turning cooler and the last of the fresh corn is making its way out of grocery stores. On busy days, especially, hearty soups rank highly as ideal dinners I don't have to fuss over. I might have to stir a few times, but while the chowder is simmering away on the coals, I can sit back and take in the birds in the trees, the fading sun on the horizon, and all the other things I love about being—and cooking—outside.

MAKES 6 SERVINGS

5 bacon slices, chopped

2 tablespoons (28 g) butter

1 yellow onion, cut into small dice

1 bell pepper, any color, cut into small dice

1 poblano pepper, cut into small dice

3 garlic cloves, minced

¼ cup (31 g) all-purpose flour

3 cups (720 ml) chicken broth

3 cups (720 ml) milk

1 tablespoon (18 g) kosher salt, plus more for seasoning

½ teaspoon ground black pepper

½ teaspoon smoked paprika, plus more for serving

4 ears corn, shucked, kernels cut off the cobs (4 to 4½ cups, or 616 to 693 g, kernels)

1 pound (454 g) red or gold potatoes, cut into small dice

½ cup (120 ml) heavy cream

Chopped scallions, white and green parts, for serving

Prepare a mound of wood coals or hardwood lump charcoal (see page 12).

Move about 2 quarts' worth (400 g) of coals to the cooking pit and arrange them in a full spread (see page 120). Place a well-seasoned Dutch oven over the coals and preheat for 10 minutes.

Add the bacon. Cook for about 5 minutes, until browned and crisp, stirring occasionally.

Add the butter, stirring until melted. Add the onion, bell pepper, and poblano. Cook for about 5 minutes, until softened, stirring occasionally. Add the garlic. Cook until fragrant, about 30 seconds. Sprinkle in the flour and stir until the vegetables are evenly coated and no lumps remain.

Pour in the chicken broth and milk. Add the salt, pepper, and smoked paprika. Cover the Dutch oven with a lid and bring to a boil.

Replenish the coals, if needed, to maintain the heat. Add the corn and potatoes. Re-cover the pot and bring to a lively simmer. Cook for 15 to 20 minutes, until the potatoes are soft.

Stir in the heavy cream until well blended. Taste and add more salt, if desired. Garnish the chowder with scallions and sprinkle each bowl with smoked paprika before serving.

2 tablespoons (30 ml) olive oil

8 ounces (225 g) boneless chicken thighs, cut into ½-inch (1 cm) chunks

8 ounces (225 g) andouille sausage, halved lengthwise and thinly sliced into half-moons

2 bell peppers, any color, cut into small dice

2 celery stalks, cut into small dice

1 onion, cut into small dice

1 tablespoon (7.5 g) Cajun Creole Spice Blend (page 111)

1 tablespoon (16 g) tomato paste

2 teaspoons Louisiana-style hot sauce, plus more for serving

½ teaspoon kosher salt

3 cups (720 ml) chicken broth, plus more as needed

1 (14-ounce, or 395 g) can diced tomatoes, undrained

2 garlic cloves, minced

2 bay leaves

1 cup (185 g) uncooked long-grain white rice

8 ounces (225 g) medium shrimp, peeled and deveined

4 scallions, white and green parts, thinly sliced

DUTCH OVEN JAMBALAYA

After college, while driving cross-country to start my new adult life, I decided to stop in New Orleans. Ever since, I've been smitten with eating and cooking Louisiana cuisine (see page 131 for my favorite gumbo recipe). Jambalaya has long been a favorite in my repertoire of Southern recipes, as I love the savory and spicy blend of flavors, the ease of preparation, and the one-pot aspect. But, most of all, I just really love stuffing my face into a big bowl of comfort, and jambalaya—a satiating mix of rice, meats, and vegetables infused with assertive herbs and spices—is exactly that.

MAKES 4 SERVINGS

Prepare a mound of wood coals or hardwood lump charcoal (see page 12).

Move about 1 quart's worth (200 g) of coals to the cooking pit and arrange them in a ring (see page 120). Place a well-seasoned Dutch oven over the coals and preheat for 10 minutes.

Swirl the olive oil into the pot. Add the chicken in a single layer. Cook, undisturbed, for 3 to 4 minutes, until browned on the bottom. Push the chicken to the sides of the Dutch oven and add the sausage. Cook, undisturbed, for 3 to 4 minutes more.

Add the bell peppers, celery, and onion. Cook for 8 to 10 minutes, until the vegetables start to soften, stirring occasionally and scraping the browned bits from the bottom of the Dutch oven. Stir in the Cajun Creole spice blend, tomato paste, hot sauce, and salt until well combined.

RECIPE CONTINUES

Put another quart's worth (200 g) of coals under the Dutch oven and arrange them in a full spread (see page 120). Pour in the chicken broth and tomatoes and their juice. Add the garlic and bay leaves. Cover the pot with a lid and bring to a simmer.

Stir in the rice and return the mixture to a simmer. Continue cooking, uncovered, for about 18 minutes, until the rice is just about done, stirring occasionally. Depending on the heat of your fire, the rice may stick to the bottom before it's fully cooked; if this happens, add a splash of broth, as needed, to keep the rice from scorching.

Stir in the shrimp. Cook for about 2 minutes, until the flesh is opaque and just cooked through. Remove the Dutch oven from the heat and stir in the scallions.

Remove and discard the bay leaves before serving. Pass hot sauce at the table for guests to add more to taste.

FIRESIDE CHICKEN AND SMOKED SAUSAGE GUMBO

Remember what I said about Louisiana cooking stealing my heart way back when? (Read about my Dutch Oven Jambalaya on page 128.) This recipe has been in regular rotation in my kitchen for more than fifteen years, and it's still going strong! Because of the roux, gumbo is a little more time-consuming to make compared to jamba-laya, but all that effort is worth it once you sit down next to a crackling fire and have your first bite. It's the perfect cool-weather meal to make when summery salads and skewers on the grill start transitioning into soups and stews in a cast iron pot.

The trick to making gumbo over a bed of coals is making the roux on the stovetop first to ensure it doesn't burn, as burnt roux means starting over from scratch. The roux can be added to the gumbo as it cooks to thicken the stew and deepen the flavor.

MAKES 6 SERVINGS

FOR THE ROUX

½ cup (120 ml) canola oil

¾ cup (93 g) all-purpose flour

FOR THE GUMBO

1 pound (454 g) boneless, skinless chicken thighs, cut into ½-inch (1 cm) chunks

Kosher salt

½ teaspoon ground black pepper, plus more for seasoning

2 tablespoons (30 ml) canola oil

2 yellow onions, cut into small dice

2 bell peppers, any color, cut into small dice

2 celery stalks, cut into small dice

4 garlic cloves, minced

1 teaspoon dried basil

1 teaspoon dried thyme

1 teaspoon dried oregano

½ teaspoon cayenne pepper

2 bay leaves

6 cups (1.4 L) chicken broth

8 ounces (225 g) andouille sausage, halved lengthwise and sliced into half-moons

2 cups (600 g) sliced okra

Cooked white rice, for serving

Thinly sliced scallion, white and green parts, for garnishing

Louisiana-style hot sauce, for serving

RECIPE CONTINUES

Prepare a mound of wood coals or hardwood lump charcoal (see page 12).

Meanwhile, to make the roux on the stovetop: In a small saucepan over medium heat, combine the canola oil and flour. Cook, whisking constantly and scraping the sides and bottom of the saucepan to prevent scorching, until the mixture is smooth and darkened to a deep peanut butter color, about 15 minutes. (Be careful not to burn the roux, as you'll have to discard it and start over.) Remove the roux from the heat. Set aside until needed.

To make the gumbo: Generously season the chicken with salt and pepper. Set aside.

Move about 2 quarts' worth (400 g) of coals to the cooking pit and arrange them in a full spread (see page 120). Place a well-seasoned Dutch oven over the coals and preheat for 10 minutes.

Drizzle the canola oil into the Dutch oven. Add the onions, bell peppers, and celery. Season with a few pinches of salt and pepper. Cook for 8 to 10 minutes, until the vegetables are tender, stirring occasionally. Sprinkle in the garlic, basil, thyme, oregano, cayenne, ½ teaspoon of black pepper, and bay leaves and stir to combine. Cook for 5 minutes.

Give the roux a few turns with a whisk and stir it into the vegetables until evenly coated. Add the chicken broth, chicken, sausage, and okra. Cover the Dutch oven with a lid. Bring the gumbo to a simmer and cook for 15 minutes, stirring occasionally. Taste and add more salt and pepper, if desired.

Serve the gumbo over bowls of rice and garnish with scallions. Pass hot sauce at the table for guests to add more to taste.

BACON AND CHORIZO HASH WITH SWEET CORN, PEPPERS, AND POTATOES

Hash is one of those "anything goes" meals that falls in the same category as frittatas, scrambles, and soups—if there's anything left over in the fridge at the end of the week, it goes in a hash. Run out of potatoes? Try half baby potatoes and half sweet potatoes. No chorizo? Use your favorite sausage instead. Want to mix up the vegetables? Tomatoes, mushrooms, and zucchini are all fair game. There are few things that wouldn't taste great when cooked in a hearty bed of bacon and potatoes, and the fact that it all cooks in one pan is a win! (Triple win if you serve up a steaming hot skillet of hash with grilled toast and a round of bloody marys.)

MAKES 6 SERVINGS

4 ears corn, shucked

Olive oil cooking spray, for misting

8 ounces (225 g) thick-cut bacon, chopped

8 ounces (225 g) Mexican chorizo, casing removed

1 yellow onion, diced

1 pound (454 g) baby potatoes, diced

1 bell pepper, any color, diced

1 jalapeño pepper, minced

Finely chopped fresh cilantro, for garnishing

Prepare a medium-hot single-level fire in a charcoal grill (see page 13) with a grill grate over the coals.

Mist the corn with cooking spray. Arrange it on the grate and close the grill lid. Grill for 6 to 8 minutes, turning occasionally, until the corn begins to soften and char. Transfer the corn to a cutting board.

Place a well-seasoned cast iron skillet on the grate and preheat for at least 5 minutes. Meanwhile, cut the kernels off the cobs. Set aside.

Add the bacon to the skillet. Cook for about 5 minutes, until crisp and the fat has rendered, stirring occasionally. Drain the bacon grease, reserving 1 tablespoon (15 ml) in the skillet along with the cooked bacon.

Return the skillet to the grate and add the chorizo and onion. Cook for about 2 minutes, until the onion turns translucent. Stir in the corn kernels, potatoes, bell pepper, and jalapeño and close the grill lid. Continue cooking for 5 to 10 minutes, stirring occasionally, until the potatoes are tender.

Garnish with cilantro before serving.

HOT TIP

Keep a sheet pan handy when you make this recipe. When you need to drain the bacon grease, you can pour it off onto the sheet pan, which is much easier than aiming a hot and heavy cast iron skillet into a saucepan.

JUICY JUMBO CREOLE SHRIMP

Get your napkins ready, because this dish is best eaten with your fingers from start to finish! Luscious shrimp in the shell are simmered in a buttery, spicy, tomato-y broth that's good enough to eat on its own. And you certainly can—but I love having a loaf of French bread on hand to soak up all the juices. For variation, serve it over rice or noodles. I don't recommend taking a shortcut with peeled shrimp here, as the shells add a nice depth of flavor to the dipping broth.

MAKES 4 SERVINGS

2 cups (480 ml) seafood stock

1 cup (240 ml) pilsner or pale lager

3 tablespoons (48 g) tomato paste

2 tablespoons (15 g) Cajun Creole Spice Blend (page 111)

Juice of 1 lemon

1 tablespoon (15 ml) Worcestershire sauce

1 tablespoon (15 ml) Louisiana-style hot sauce, plus more as needed

1 teaspoon ground black pepper

2 garlic cloves, minced

2 pounds (908 g) jumbo shrimp, tail-on and unpeeled

8 tablespoons (1 stick, or 112 g) butter, cut into small cubes

Kosher salt

Crusty French bread, for serving

Prepare a hot single-level fire in a fire pit or charcoal grill (see page 13) with a grill grate over the coals. Place a well-seasoned cast iron skillet on the grate and preheat for at least 5 minutes.

In the hot skillet, combine the seafood stock, pilsner, tomato paste, Cajun Creole spice blend, lemon juice, Worcestershire sauce, hot sauce, pepper, and garlic. Stir to combine. Cover the skillet with a lid and bring the ingredients to a simmer. Simmer for about 15 minutes, until the sauce is fragrant and well blended.

Add the shrimp and stir to coat with the sauce. Cook for 5 to 10 minutes, until the shrimp are opaque and just cooked through, stirring occasionally.

Remove the skillet from the heat. Scatter the butter over the shrimp and stir to melt the cubes into the sauce. Taste and season with salt or add more hot sauce, as desired. Serve with crusty bread to sop up all the broth.

HOT TIP

Make the Cajun Creole Spice Blend (page 111) a staple in your spice pantry! You can also use it in my Dutch Oven Jambalaya (page 128) or Spicy Smoked Sausage, Snap Beans, and Potatoes (page 110).

ONE-PAN SEAFOOD AND SMOKED GOUDA FETTUCCINE

So why would one make pasta on the grill instead of the stovetop? The magic ingredient here is one you can't replicate in your kitchen—the fragrant smoke that swirls around a charcoal grill. It infuses the seafood with a deeper layer of flavor and rounds out the richness of the smoked Gouda, essentially becoming a seasoning of its own. I like to use a mix of shrimp and scallops in this dish, but you can also try white fish fillets, clams, or mussels.

MAKES 4 SERVINGS

8 asparagus spears, woody ends trimmed

Olive oil cooking spray, for misting

1 pound (454 g) mixed seafood

½ teaspoon kosher salt, plus more for seasoning

Ground black pepper

2 cups (480 ml) milk

1½ cups (360 ml) chicken broth, plus more as needed

2 tablespoons (28 g) butter

2 garlic cloves, minced

8 ounces (225 g) dried fettuccine

½ cup (120 ml) heavy cream

¼ cup (30 g) grated smoked Gouda cheese, plus more for serving

Minced fresh parsley, for garnishing

Prepare a hot two-zone fire in a charcoal grill (see page 13) with a grill grate over the coals.

Lightly mist the asparagus with cooking spray and arrange it on the grate over direct heat. Grill the asparagus for 6 to 8 minutes, turning occasionally, until tender and lightly charred. Transfer to a cutting board.

Place a well-seasoned cast iron skillet over direct heat and preheat for at least 5 minutes. While the skillet heats, cut the asparagus into 1-inch (2.5 cm) pieces and place them in a large bowl. Set aside. Thoroughly pat the seafood dry with paper towels. Mist both sides with cooking spray and season with salt and pepper.

Add the seafood to the hot skillet in a single layer. Cook for about 5 minutes, until the flesh is opaque, turning once. Transfer the seafood to the bowl of asparagus.

In the skillet, combine the milk, chicken broth, butter, garlic, and ½ teaspoon of salt. Cover the skillet with a lid and bring to a simmer. When the butter is fully melted, add the fettuccine. Re-cover the skillet and return the mixture to a simmer. Cook for 3 to 5 minutes, stirring the pasta frequently to separate the strands, until softened. Remove the lid, give it a stir to ensure all the strands are spread evenly across the skillet, and close the grill lid.

RECIPE CONTINUES

Continue simmering for 8 to 10 minutes, uncovered and with the grill lid closed, stirring occasionally, until the pasta is almost cooked but there is still some liquid at the bottom. (If the liquid is reducing more quickly than the pasta can cook, add a splash of broth and move the skillet to the cooler side of the grill to adjust the rate of simmer.)

Stir in the heavy cream and Gouda. Simmer, uncovered, for 1 to 2 minutes, until the sauce is thickened and the pasta is fully cooked. Taste and add more salt, if desired.

Add the asparagus and seafood. Toss to combine and cook until warmed through. Serve the pasta with a sprinkle of parsley and more Gouda on top.

SPATCHCOCKED CHICKEN UNDER A SKILLET

I'll admit it, "spatchcock" is simply a fun word to say! Linguistics aside, it's also the best way to cook a whole bird if you want to attain the Holy Grail of grilled chicken—crispy skin, juicy breasts, and tender thighs all at the same time. Spatchcocking involves butterflying a whole chicken by removing the backbone (which is easier than it sounds, and much easier after your first time) so the meat lies flat and cooks more evenly. The classic Italian method (pollo al mattone) uses bricks to weight the chicken down for an all-over char on the skin; in this recipe, I use what I always have around—a heavy cast iron skillet.

You can try any combination of herbs in this recipe; in fact, I sometimes call it "fresh-from-the-garden marinade" (or perhaps more often, "leftover-herbs-in-the-back-of-the-fridge marinade") because I've never gone wrong with any handful of fresh, fragrant herbs. My favorites are thyme, oregano, rosemary, parsley, and cilantro—sometimes just a few, and sometimes all at once.

MAKES 4 SERVINGS

1 (4-pound, or 1.8 kg) whole chicken, giblets removed, patted dry with paper towels

½ cup (120 ml) olive oil

Zest and juice of 1 lemon

⅓ cup (weight varies) mixed minced fresh herbs

2 garlic cloves, minced

¼ teaspoon red pepper flakes

Kosher salt

Ground black pepper

1 lemon, halved crosswise

RECIPE CONTINUES

Step 1

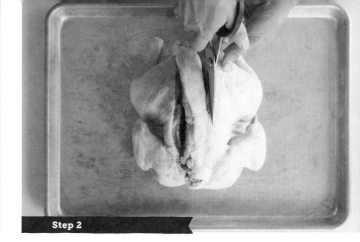

Step 2

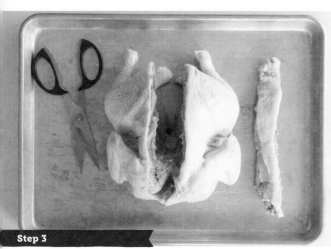

Step 3

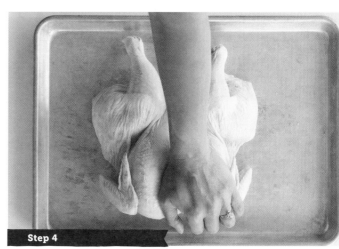

Step 4

Step 5

A Spatchcocked Chicken

Want the fastest and easiest way to cook a Thanksgiving turkey? Spatchcock it! The same principle of evenly cooked, juicy meat and browned, crispy skin when the bird is splayed on the grill applies to turkeys as well. While you won't get the traditional presentation of a whole turkey on the table, you'll free up your oven and have the turkey grilled, rested, and carved in only 2 hours—a fair trade, in my opinion!

In general, a 22-inch (55 cm) kettle grill can accommodate a 10- to 12-pound (4.5 to 5.4 kg) spatchcocked turkey. Grill it over indirect medium-high heat for about 1½ hours, until the breast registers 150°F (66°C) and the thigh registers 170°F (77°C) on an instant-read thermometer. Bonus: the removed turkey backbone makes excellent gravy!

NOT JUST A FUN WORD TO SAY . . .

Where did the term *spatchcock* come from? Though up for debate, one theory from the folks at *Oxford English Dictionary* is the word has Irish origins, and is an abbreviation of "dispatch cock," a phrase referring to fowl "split open and grilled after being killed, plucked, and dressed in a summary fashion."

TO SPATCHCOCK THE CHICKEN:

1. Place the chicken, breast-side down, on a cutting board so the chicken's back is facing up. Using heavy-duty kitchen or poultry shears, start at the cavity next to the thigh and cut along one side of the backbone to the neck.

2. Cut along the other side of the backbone.

3. Completely remove the backbone (discard it or save it for stock).

4. Flip the chicken, breast-side up, and firmly flatten it with the palm of your hand to crack the breastbone.

5. Cut off the wing tips and discard (or save for stock).

In a small bowl, whisk the olive oil, lemon zest, lemon juice, herbs, garlic, and red pepper flakes until combined. Place the chicken in a baking dish and pour the marinade over the chicken. Rub the marinade all over the skin until evenly coated. Cover and refrigerate for at least 2 hours, or overnight.

Prepare a medium-hot two-zone fire in a charcoal grill (see page 13) with a grill grate over the coals. Cover the outside bottom of a cast iron skillet with foil. Set aside until ready to use.

Lift the chicken out of the marinade and let the excess oil drip off. Liberally season the chicken with salt and pepper. Place the chicken, skin-side down, on the grate over direct heat with the breasts facing the cooler side of the grill. Place the prepared skillet on top of the chicken to weight it down and close the grill lid. Grill for 10 to 15 minutes, until the skin is brown and crisp.

Remove the skillet, flip the chicken, and move it over indirect heat with the legs facing the hotter side of the grill. Close the grill lid. Grill for 20 to 30 minutes, until an instant-read thermometer inserted into the thickest part of the breast reads 160°F (71°C). (For extra crispy skin, you can flip it one more time, skin-side down, over direct heat for a few minutes more.) Transfer the chicken to a cutting board and let rest for 10 minutes.

Place the lemon halves, cut-side down, on the grill over direct heat. Grill for about 5 minutes, until the edges are charred.

Carve and serve the chicken with a squeeze of charred lemon on top.

GRIDDLED FRENCH TOAST ROLLS WITH BLUEBERRIES AND CREAM

I love finding interesting new ways to make and serve old favorites, like French toast. This variation uses a loaf of sandwich bread—just plain ol' white bread, and fresh bread at that—to turn the traditional toast into French toast roll-ups stuffed with blueberry preserves. The whole batch cooks at once on a plancha so everyone can enjoy them while they're hot and toasty. (That's a real sticking point for me when it comes to making breakfast items such as French toast and pancakes—be sure to check out my Dutch Oven–Baked Buttermilk Pancake with Raspberries and Almonds, page 124, if you feel the same way!)

Don't skimp on the velvety whipped cream by using store-bought. The crème fraîche adds just the right amount of tang to cut through the sweetness of the French toast and it gives the cream extra body and smoothness, almost like eating clouds.

MAKES 4 SERVINGS

FOR THE WHIPPED CREAM

¼ cup (56 g) crème fraîche

2 tablespoons (15 g) confectioners' sugar

1 cup (240 ml) heavy cream

FOR THE FRENCH TOAST

2 large eggs, beaten

⅓ cup (80 ml) milk

2 tablespoons (25 g) granulated sugar

½ teaspoon ground cinnamon

¼ teaspoon kosher salt

16 slices soft white sandwich bread, crusts removed

Blueberry preserves, for spreading

2 tablespoons (28 g) butter

1½ cups (220 g) fresh blueberries

Maple syrup, for serving (optional)

To make the whipped cream: At least 30 minutes before you plan to make the whipped cream, place a large deep bowl and large balloon whisk in the freezer to chill. You want to start with very cold tools and ingredients for successfully whipping the cream. Alternatively, if using a handheld electric mixer, stand mixer, or high-powered blender, there is no need to freeze the whisk or bowl.

In a small bowl, using a fork, mix together the crème fraîche and confectioners' sugar until combined.

In the chilled bowl, using the chilled whisk (or using an unchilled bowl with the handheld mixer, stand mixer, or blender on medium to medium-high speed) beat the heavy cream until stiff peaks form. Using a rubber spatula, gently fold the crème fraîche into the whipped cream until smooth and blended. Cover and refrigerate until ready to serve.

To make the French toast: Prepare a medium single-level fire in a fire pit or charcoal grill (see page 13) with a grill grate over the coals.

In a medium bowl, whisk the eggs, milk, granulated sugar, cinnamon, and salt until well blended. Set aside until needed.

RECIPE CONTINUES

Using a rolling pin, roll out each slice of bread to ⅛ inch (0.3 cm) thickness. Spread a thin layer of blueberry preserves on each slice of bread and roll each tightly into a cylinder, up and away from you. Dip each roll into the egg mixture until lightly coated on all sides.

Place a well-seasoned plancha on the grate and preheat for at least 5 minutes.

On the plancha, melt the butter, spreading it around to evenly coat the surface. Arrange the rolls in a single layer on the plancha. Cook until all four sides are golden brown, 1 to 2 minutes per side.

Remove the whipped cream from the fridge and give it a few turns with a whisk.

Serve the French toast rolls with a dollop of whipped cream, a handful of fresh blueberries, and maple syrup for dipping (if desired).

CHARRED EDAMAME WITH CHILE-GARLIC SAUCE

Edamame are one of those finger foods that are strangely meditative and addictive to eat. There's something so satisfying about bringing a pod to your lips, sucking on the end, and popping a bean into your mouth—then doing it again, and again. And this appetizer is one you'll probably want to make a double batch of, as it tends to go quickly at parties! Grilling edamame on a plancha (rather than simply steaming them) adds a subtle hint of smoke you won't find in traditional preparations, and the creamy garlicky sauce has a little kick without overwhelming your taste buds.

MAKES 4 SERVINGS

1 tablespoon (15 g) sambal oelek (Asian chile paste; see recipe note)

1 tablespoon (14 g) mayonnaise

1 tablespoon (15 ml) soy sauce

2 garlic cloves, crushed

1 pound (454 g) fresh edamame in pods, or frozen and thawed

Olive oil cooking spray, for misting

Kosher salt

Prepare a hot single-level fire in a fire pit or charcoal grill (see page 13) with a grill grate over the coals. Place a well-seasoned plancha on the grate and preheat for at least 5 minutes.

In a small bowl, stir together the sambal oelek, mayonnaise, soy sauce, and garlic. Set aside.

Lightly mist the edamame with cooking spray. Spread the edamame across the plancha in a single layer. Grill, undisturbed, for about 3 minutes, until lightly charred on the bottom. Toss and grill for about 2 minutes more, until tender. Transfer the edamame to a serving bowl and toss with the chile-garlic sauce until coated. Serve with a sprinkle of salt on top.

RECIPE NOTE
Sambal oelek can be found in the Asian foods aisle of most well-stocked supermarkets. It's sometimes labeled as ground fresh chile paste or chili garlic sauce (Huy Fong is a common brand).

SEARED SCALLOPS WITH GINGER-LIME BUTTER

Scallops on the grill are one of my favorite "gourmet" meals to make, even though they're astonishingly simple to pull off—and tough to mess up if you grill them on a plancha. The smoking-hot cast iron surface helps the scallops form a desirable brown crust, which complements their naturally buttery texture. In this dish, they're topped with a fragrant sauce that starts out gingery and zesty and finishes with a sweet, mellow spice. I sometimes serve smaller portions as a first course to get my guests excited for what's to come!

MAKES 4 SERVINGS

8 tablespoons (1 stick, or 112 g) butter

1 Fresno chile pepper, minced

2 garlic cloves, crushed

1 tablespoon (8 g) grated peeled fresh ginger

Juice of 1 lime

1 tablespoon (1 g) minced fresh cilantro

24 (U15) sea scallops (about 1½ pounds, or 681 g; see recipe note)

Olive oil cooking spray, for misting

Kosher salt

Ground black pepper

Zest of 1 lime

Prepare a hot single-level fire in a fire pit or charcoal grill (see page 13) with a grill grate over the coals. Place a well-seasoned plancha on the grate and preheat for at least 5 minutes.

On the stovetop, in a small saucepan over medium heat, combine the butter, chile pepper, garlic, ginger, and lime juice. Cook, stirring frequently, until the butter melts and the mixture is well blended. Remove from the heat and stir in the cilantro. Set aside until needed.

Thoroughly pat the scallops dry with paper towels. Mist them on both sides with cooking spray and season with salt and pepper. Arrange the scallops on the plancha, being careful not to crowd them. Grill for about 3 minutes, until the bottoms have a deep brown crust. Turn the scallops over and grill until the flesh is opaque and firm, 2 to 3 minutes more.

Divide the scallops among four serving plates. Drizzle the sauce over the scallops and add a sprinkle of lime zest on top before serving.

RECIPE NOTE
A U15 designation indicates there are 15 or fewer scallops per pound (454 g).

DECONSTRUCTED BLT SALAD

Lettuce is probably not the first thing that comes to mind when you think "grilling," but it's one of my favorite vegetables to put on the grill because the high heat transforms it from bland and boring to something much more interesting. (Brushing it with bacon fat doesn't hurt either.) If you're looking for a new take on salad for your next barbecue, this is it!

MAKES 6 TO 8 SERVINGS

FOR THE DRESSING

¼ cup (60 g) mayonnaise

¼ cup (60 ml) buttermilk

3 tablespoons (45 ml) distilled white vinegar

2 tablespoons (6 g) minced fresh chives

Kosher salt

Ground black pepper

FOR THE SALAD

1 pound (454 g) tomatoes, cut into ½-inch (1 cm) wedges

Kosher salt

6 thick-cut bacon slices

6 (½-inch, or 1 cm) slices French bread

2 hearts of romaine lettuce, halved lengthwise, root end intact

Ground black pepper

Prepare a medium-hot single-level fire in a fire pit or charcoal grill (see page 13) with a grill grate over the coals. Place a well-seasoned plancha on the grate and preheat for at least 5 minutes.

To make the dressing: In a bowl large enough to hold the salad, whisk all the dressing ingredients until combined. Set aside.

To make the salad: Season the tomatoes with salt and place them in a colander. Let drain while you grill the remaining ingredients.

Arrange the bacon on the plancha. Cook for 2 to 3 minutes per side, until browned and crisp. Transfer the bacon to paper towels to drain. Slice into ½-inch (1 cm) strips. Remove the plancha from the grill and reserve the bacon grease.

Lightly brush the bread with the bacon grease and arrange it on the grate. Grill for about 30 seconds per side, until toasted with good grill marks. Transfer the bread to a cutting board and cut into ½-inch (1 cm) chunks.

Lightly brush the lettuce with bacon grease and season with salt and pepper. Place the lettuce on the grate, cut-side down, and grill for about 2 minutes, until charred on the outside but still crisp and raw inside. Turn the lettuce over and grill until the outer leaves are slightly wilted, 1 to 2 minutes. Transfer the lettuce to a cutting board. Trim and discard the ends and slice the lettuce crosswise into ½-inch (1 cm) strips.

Add the bacon, bread, lettuce, and tomatoes to the bowl with the dressing. Immediately before serving, gently toss the salad until combined and evenly coated with dressing.

HOT HOAGIES

These classic Italian sandwiches (which you may know as hoagies, heros, subs, or torpedos, depending on where you're from) are a flavorful step up from the beloved campfire hot dog. They're also simple to make, and the forgiving nature of grilling on a plancha means you don't have to worry too much about burning your food. I like my hoagies piled high with peppers and onions; any leftover vegetables can be tossed in a scramble or served in a rice bowl the next day.

MAKES 6 SERVINGS

⅓ cup (80 ml) olive oil

2 tablespoons (30 ml) balsamic vinegar

3 bell peppers, any color, cut into thin strips

1 yellow onion, thinly sliced

Olive oil cooking spray, for preparing the vegetables

Kosher salt

Ground black pepper

6 hot Italian sausage links

6 thin slices provolone cheese

6 Italian-style hoagie rolls or brat buns

Homemade Giardiniera (page 88), for serving (optional)

Prepare a hot single-level fire in a fire pit or charcoal grill (see page 13) with a grill grate over the coals. Place a well-seasoned plancha on the grate and preheat for at least 5 minutes.

In a large bowl, whisk the olive oil and vinegar until blended. Set aside.

Lightly spray the bell peppers and onion with cooking spray and season with a few pinches each of salt and pepper. Spread the vegetables across the plancha. Grill for 10 to 15 minutes, tossing occasionally with tongs, until softened and reduced in volume by one-third. (I like to let the vegetables cook undisturbed for a few minutes to brown the bottoms a bit.) Transfer the vegetables to the bowl with the vinaigrette and toss to coat. Set aside until needed.

Arrange the sausages on the plancha. Grill for 8 to 10 minutes, turning occasionally, until browned all over and cooked through. An instant-read thermometer inserted into the center of the sausages should read 160°F (71°C).

Lay 1 slice of cheese inside each roll. Place the rolls on the plancha. Toast until lightly browned and warmed through, 1 to 2 minutes per side.

To serve, tuck a sausage into each roll and add a heap of peppers and onions. Pass around the giardiniera as an additional topping, if desired.

LEMON-DILL SALMON A LA PLANCHA

On a plancha, these meaty salmon steaks sear in their own juices, concentrate all that zippy flavor from the lemon and dill dressing, and develop a mouthwatering crust without the downsides of cooking fish on a grill. (You know— the agony of burning, sticking, and leaving half the flesh on the grate.) The key to picture-perfect salmon is waiting for that crust to form; don't flip too early because, as the flesh turns crackly and golden brown, the fish will release easily from the plancha.

MAKES 4 SERVINGS

¼ cup (60 ml) olive oil

2 tablespoons (30 ml) dry white wine

2 tablespoons (8 g) minced fresh dill

2 tablespoons (30 ml) fresh lemon juice

Zest of 1 lemon

4 (8-ounce, or 225 g, 1½-inch, or 3.5 cm, -thick) salmon steaks

Kosher salt

Ground black pepper

1 lemon, thinly sliced

Prepare a hot single-level fire in a charcoal grill (see page 13) with a grill grate over the coals. Place a well-seasoned plancha on the grate and preheat for at least 5 minutes.

In a small bowl, whisk the olive oil, wine, dill, lemon juice, and lemon zest. Set aside one-third of the sauce. Generously brush the remaining sauce on both sides of the salmon and season it with salt and pepper.

Arrange the salmon on the plancha and close the grill lid. Grill, undisturbed, for about 5 minutes. Turn the salmon over and re-close the grill lid. Grill for about 5 minutes more, until an instant-read thermometer inserted into the thickest part of the flesh reaches 120°F to 125°F (49°C to 52°C).

Arrange a few lemon slices on each serving plate and place the salmon on top. Add a heaping spoonful of the reserved lemon-dill sauce over each salmon before serving.

GRILLED PORK MEDALLIONS WITH CHERRY-BOURBON SAUCE

Tenderloins are one of my favorite cuts of pork, and these medallions (just a frilly term for sliced tenderloin) stay true to their name, turning oh so tender and incredibly juicy on the grill. The key to not overcooking the meat is searing it over direct heat to get a good char, and finishing over indirect heat. A sweet and savory cherry sauce spiked with bourbon—which we cook right on the grill grate while the pork rests—makes this deceptively fancy meal seem like you put a lot more work into it than you actually did.

MAKES 4 SERVINGS

FOR THE PORK

2 (1-pound, or 454 g) pork tenderloins, trimmed of excess fat

Kosher salt

Ground black pepper

FOR THE SAUCE

4 tablespoons (½ stick, or 56 g) butter

½ shallot, finely chopped

1 pound (454 g) sweet cherries, pitted and halved

¼ cup (60 ml) bourbon

2 tablespoons (30 ml) balsamic vinegar

2 thyme sprigs, leaves stripped

Prepare a medium-hot two-zone fire in a charcoal grill (see page 13) with a grill grate over the coals.

To make the pork: Liberally season the pork with salt and pepper. Place the pork on the grate over direct heat. Sear for about 2 minutes on all four sides, until evenly charred. Move the pork over indirect heat and close the grill lid. Grill for about 4 minutes on each of the wider sides, until an instant-read thermometer inserted into the center reaches 140°F (60°C). Transfer the pork to a cutting board, tent with aluminum foil, and let rest while you prepare the sauce.

To make the sauce: Preheat a well-seasoned cast iron skillet on the grate over direct heat. Add the butter to melt. Stir in the shallot. Cook for about 2 minutes, until it starts to turns translucent. Add the cherries, bourbon, and vinegar. Cook for 5 to 7 minutes until the cherries are soft and the sauce is reduced to a thin syrup. Stir in the thyme leaves and remove the skillet from the heat.

Slice the pork and serve with a few spoonfuls of sauce on top.

CHAPTER 6

FEASTING ... WITH A GRILL

You don't need an expensive grill with all the bells and whistles to turn out great food. You just need a good cover and functioning vents, two simple features that will help you make a four-star meal with more control and better timing than you'd typically get from a fire pit. By manipulating airflow in a tighter environment, you can use your grill for high-heat searing as well as slow roasting and baking. Nearly anything you can cook on the stovetop or in the oven, you can cook on the grill.

Start with a midrange model when buying your first grill, and choose one that's a little larger than you think you need. You don't always have to fill the whole box with coals, but you'll be glad for the extra space.

PREPARING YOUR GRILL FOR COOKING

Start with the top and bottom dampers fully open. Remove the top (cooking) grate and light your charcoal (see page 12). Once the coals are ready and raked into your desired cooking zones (see page 13), replace the top grate, close the grill lid, and let the grate preheat for about 10 minutes. Adjust the dampers as needed to hit your target temperature.

Adjusting the Temperature of Your Grill

Fire is a fickle heat source but, on a grill, you can tame the flames with little effort once you learn to use the dampers (or vents).

The dampers control the amount of air that flows through the grill. Air is your friend when it comes to starting and maintaining a fire, so, by controlling the airflow, you control the heat.

The bottom damper brings oxygen to the fire. The top damper acts as a chimney, creating a draft that pulls heat and smoke out of your grill. Opening the dampers allows more air to enter, meaning more heat; closing the dampers means less air and less heat. Remember the cardinal rule of venting: **close to cool, open to heat**. Adjust the vents in tandem and give the fire time to react in order to reach its final temperature. Keep in mind that closing and opening the grill lid can affect the temperature gauge, so it's not always an accurate measure of heat.

It takes some practice to figure out the ideal damper settings for your grill but, in most circumstances, you can leave the top and bottom dampers partially open to maintain temperatures between 300°F and 500°F (150°C and 260°C). I typically leave my bottom damper in one position while I adjust the top damper; this method often gets me within 5°F to 10°F (2°C to 4°C) of the needed temperature.

If you still have charcoal remaining after a grill session, close the top and bottom dampers to choke the fire. You can save and use the unburned charcoal next time.

Caring for Your Grill

A little goes a long way when it comes to grill maintenance. Get into the habit of doing a few simple tasks each time you grill, and you'll save yourself a lot of elbow grease, time, and money at the end of the season.

Every grill session:

+ Empty the ash catcher.

+ Clean and oil the grate *before* and *after* you grill.

+ If inclement weather is forecast, cover the grill with a waterproof cover or store it indoors.

Once every few months:

+ Deep clean the grates and the inside and outside of your grill once a season to prevent buildup of soot and grease.

+ Lubricate the dampers with WD-40 if they feel sticky.

BRUNCH PIZZA WITH PANCETTA, PESTO, AND EGGS

Eggs on pizza. It's one of my favorite combinations because I love my eggs sunny-side up, and I love when the yolks spill over and create their own sauce. Even though this recipe has a tiny ingredient list, it is surprisingly big on flavor, thanks to the salty pancetta, fragrant pesto, and rich, runny yolks. Make the dough the night before so you'll be ready to go the next morning!

MAKES 4 SERVINGS

1 pound (454 g) Homemade Pizza Dough (page 163) or store-bought pizza dough

8 ounces (225 g) pancetta, cut into ¼-inch (0.6 cm) dice, or smaller

Olive oil cooking spray, for misting

½ cup (130 g) Homemade Basil-Walnut Pesto (page 162) or store-bought pesto

2 cups (230 g) shredded Colby Jack cheese

4 large eggs

Bring the chilled pizza dough to room temperature for at least 30 minutes.

Prepare a hot two-zone fire in a charcoal grill (see page 13) with a grill grate over the coals.

Meanwhile, heat a medium skillet on the stovetop over medium-high heat. Add the pancetta. Cook for about 5 minutes, until brown and crispy. Set aside until ready to use.

Divide the dough in half and shape it into 2 smooth balls. Working with the first dough ball, flatten it into a disk and roll into an 8-inch (20 cm) round. Prick the dough all over with a fork and lightly mist the surface with cooking spray.

Place the dough, oiled-side down, on the grate over direct heat. Grill for about 2 minutes, until the bottom is lightly browned and the crust is barely cooked on top. Mist the top of the crust with cooking spray and turn it over.

Working quickly, spread half the pesto on the crust (all the way to the edges), followed by half each of the cheese and pancetta. Crack 2 eggs onto the pizza. (If the crust seems to be burning before you can load up all the toppings, slide it to the cooler side of the grill while you finish.)

Move the pizza over indirect heat and close the grill lid. Continue grilling until the egg whites are set but the yolks are still slightly runny, 5 to 7 minutes.

Repeat the process to make the second pizza.

HOMEMADE BASIL-WALNUT PESTO

Fresh and earthy, this pesto leans toward the traditional side but uses rich, buttery walnuts in place of pine nuts. A squeeze of lemon at the end adds brightness.

MAKES 1 CUP (260 G)

2 cups (70 g) packed fresh basil

½ cup (50 g) grated Parmesan cheese

⅓ cup (50 g) walnuts

3 garlic cloves, peeled

½ teaspoon kosher salt

¼ to ⅓ cup (60 to 80 ml) olive oil

Squeeze of fresh lemon juice

In a food processor, combine the basil, cheese, walnuts, garlic, and salt. Pulse to combine, scraping down the sides of the bowl with a rubber spatula as needed. With the processor running on low speed, add the olive oil in a slow, steady stream until the mixture becomes a smooth, thin, spreadable paste. (If you are making pesto to use as a sauce or drizzle for other recipes, feel free to add up to ¼ cup [60 ml] more oil for a thinner consistency.)

Transfer the pesto to an airtight container and stir in a squeeze of lemon juice. Refrigerate for up to 1 week, or freeze for 6 to 9 months.

HOMEMADE PIZZA DOUGH

When you see how simple it is to make your own dough, you may never go back to buying prepared pizza dough or premade crusts from the store. Use this recipe for Brunch Pizza with Pancetta, Pesto, and Eggs (page 160); Thai Chicken Pizza with Sweet Chili Sauce (page 165); Three-Cheese Flatbread Pizza with Capicola and Arugula (page 166); and Peach and Prosciutto Planked Pizza (page 219).

MAKES 1 POUND (ENOUGH FOR 2 PIZZAS)

2 tablespoons (30 ml) olive oil, plus more for greasing

1 cup (240 ml) warm water (100°F to 110°F, or 38°C to 43°C)

1 teaspoon active dry yeast

1 teaspoon sugar

1 teaspoon kosher salt

½ teaspoon garlic powder

2½ cups (310 g) all-purpose flour

Lightly grease a medium bowl with olive oil and set aside.

In another medium bowl, stir together the warm water, yeast, sugar, salt, and garlic powder until combined (the ingredients do not need to be fully dissolved). Add the olive oil and flour. Using a large sturdy spoon, mix until no dry pockets remain and a loose, shaggy dough forms.

Knead the dough by hand for 3 to 5 minutes, until it looks and feels smooth. Shape the dough into a ball and lightly coat it with olive oil. Place the dough in the prepared bowl, cover with plastic wrap, and let rise at room temperature for 1 to 1½ hours, until doubled in volume.

Remove the dough from the bowl and shape it into a smooth ball. The dough is ready to use immediately.

If not using the dough the same day, tightly wrap the ball in plastic wrap and refrigerate for up to 3 days. The dough can also be frozen in a freezer bag for up to 1 month.

THAI CHICKEN PIZZA WITH SWEET CHILI SAUCE

When it comes to pizza, I like to experiment with non-tomato–based sauces (like my Brunch Pizza with Pancetta, Pesto, and Eggs, page 160) or no sauce at all (like the Peach and Prosciutto Planked Pizza, page 219). Here, I go for a Thai-inspired flavor base with sweet chili sauce, which brings out the sweetness of the bell pepper and carrot even more. To save a little time, use leftover grilled chicken or store-bought rotisserie chicken.

MAKES 4 SERVINGS

1 pound (454 g) Homemade Pizza Dough (page 163) or store-bought pizza dough

1 bell pepper, any color, halved and cored

Olive oil cooking spray, for misting

½ cup (140 g) sweet chili sauce

2 cups (230 g) shredded mozzarella cheese, plus more as desired

1 cup (140 g) cooked diced chicken

½ cup (55 g) grated carrot

¼ cup (25 g) thinly sliced scallion, white and green parts

Chopped fresh cilantro, for garnishing

Bring the chilled pizza dough to room temperature for at least 30 minutes.

Prepare a hot two-zone fire in a charcoal grill (see page 13) with a grill grate over the coals.

Lightly spray the bell pepper with cooking spray and place it on the grate over direct heat. Grill for 6 to 8 minutes, turning occasionally, until tender and lightly charred. Transfer to a cutting board and cut into thin strips.

Divide the dough in half and shape it into 2 smooth balls. Working with the first dough ball, flatten it into a disk and roll into an 8-inch (20 cm) round. Prick the dough all over with a fork and lightly mist the surface with cooking spray.

Place the dough, oiled-side down, on the grate over direct heat. Grill for about 2 minutes, until the bottom is lightly browned and the crust is barely cooked on top. Mist the top of the crust with cooking spray and turn it over.

Working quickly, spread half the sweet chili sauce on the crust (all the way to the edges), followed by half each of the mozzarella, chicken, carrot, scallion, and bell pepper. Sprinkle a little more mozzarella on top, if desired. (If the crust seems to be burning before you can load up all the toppings, slide it over to the cooler side of the grill while you finish.)

Move the pizza over indirect heat and close the grill lid. Continue grilling for 3 to 5 minutes, until the toppings are warm and the mozzarella is melted.

Repeat the process to make the second pizza.

THREE-CHEESE FLATBREAD PIZZA WITH CAPICOLA AND ARUGULA

With their smaller size and thinner crust, these flatbread pizzas are perfect for cutting into appetizer portions or serving on individual plates. Because they're sauceless, they rely on a generous spread of ricotta for their creamy texture, so use the highest quality full-fat ricotta you can find. If you want something a bit more substantial, top each pizza with an egg (à la Brunch Pizza with Pancetta, Pesto, and Eggs, page 160).

MAKES 4 SERVINGS

1 pound (454 g) Homemade Pizza Dough (page 163) or store-bought pizza dough

4 teaspoons (20 ml) olive oil

2 teaspoons balsamic vinegar

Kosher salt

Ground black pepper

2 cups (40 g) baby arugula

Olive oil cooking spray, for misting

2 cups (500 g) ricotta cheese

24 thin slices capicola (see recipe note)

1½ cups (175 g) shredded mozzarella cheese

½ cup (50 g) grated Parmesan cheese

Bring the chilled pizza dough to room temperature for at least 30 minutes.

Prepare a hot two-zone fire in a charcoal grill (see page 13) with a grill grate over the coals.

In a medium bowl, whisk the olive oil, vinegar, and a large pinch each of salt and pepper until blended. Add the arugula and toss to coat. Set aside until needed.

Divide the dough into 4 equal portions and shape each portion into a smooth ball. Flatten each dough ball into a disk and roll into an 8-inch (20 cm) round. Prick the dough all over with a fork and lightly mist the surface with cooking spray.

Working in batches, place the dough on the grate over direct heat and mist the top of the dough with cooking spray. Grill for about 2 minutes per side, until lightly browned. Transfer the finished crusts to a sheet pan.

Spread one-fourth of the ricotta evenly on each crust. Top the pizzas with one-fourth each of the capicola, mozzarella, and Parmesan. Place each pizza on the grate over indirect heat and close the grill lid. Grill for about 5 minutes, until the cheeses are melted.

Top each pizza with dressed arugula before serving.

RECIPE NOTE
Capicola, an Italian cold cut, is also labeled capocollo or coppa, and can be found in the deli section of most grocery stores.

HOT TIP

To transfer the dough to the grill while still keeping its shape, roll it out on a sheet of lightly oiled parchment paper. Prick the dough and mist the top with cooking spray. Carefully flip it over on top of the grate and peel the parchment off.

GRILLED HALLOUMI, SWEET CORN, AND TOMATO SALAD WITH BASIL VINAIGRETTE

How about a grilled cheese salad to go with all those grilled meats this summer? (Though this is not the grilled cheese you're probably thinking of!) Halloumi is a semi-hard white cheese hailing from the island of Cyprus. It has a high melting point, so it turns wonderfully creamy—not gooey—on the grill. Halloumi is comparable to a thick feta or mozzarella in texture, and while it has a salty snap right out of the package, the flavor mellows on the grill into a pleasantly savory bite. With peak-of-season ingredients like sweet corn, tomatoes, and fresh basil vinaigrette rounding out this refreshing salad, you'll find yourself bringing it to every potluck.

MAKES 4 SERVINGS

FOR THE VINAIGRETTE

½ cup (120 ml) olive oil

2 cups (70 g) packed fresh basil

½ shallot, coarsely chopped

1 garlic clove, coarsely chopped

2 tablespoons (30 ml) white wine vinegar

1 teaspoon kosher salt

FOR THE SALAD

8 ounces (225 g) halloumi, cut into ¼-inch (0.6 cm) slices

4 ears sweet corn, shucked

Olive oil cooking spray, for preparing the corn and cheese

1 pint (300 g) cherry tomatoes, halved

4 cups (284 g) mixed baby greens

Prepare a medium-hot single-level fire in a charcoal grill (see page 13) with a grill grate over the coals.

To make the vinaigrette: In a blender, combine all the vinaigrette ingredients. Purée until smooth. Set aside until ready to use.

To make the salad: Lightly spray the halloumi and corn with cooking spray. Place the halloumi on the grate. Grill for about 2 minutes per side, until charred. Arrange the corn on the grate and close the lid. Grill the corn for about 15 minutes, turning occasionally, until charred all over.

Transfer the corn and halloumi to a cutting board. Cut the kernels off the corn and slice the halloumi into small strips. Place the kernels, halloumi, tomatoes, and baby greens in a large bowl and toss to combine.

Serve the salad with a generous drizzle of vinaigrette.

HOT TIP

To keep hot kernels and juices from flying everywhere, place a small cutting board in the center of a half sheet pan. Hold the ear of corn upright and slice off the kernels with a knife. The rimmed sides of the sheet pan will contain the kernels and make it easier to collect and dump them into a bowl.

LOADED NACHOS ON THE GRILL

If there's a game on and you need something fast and easy to feed the hungry fans, these grilled nachos—loaded to the hilt with an array of awesomeness—are just the thing to tame a crowd. I actually had to hold back a little when developing this recipe because I could no longer see the chips . . . but that doesn't mean you can't add more toppings to yours! Try it with cooked ground beef, grilled shrimp, sliced fresh radishes, refried beans, shredded lettuce, guacamole, or pico de gallo for variation.

MAKES 4 SERVINGS

½ cup (68 g) Pickled Jalapeños (page 172)

1 cup (149 g) grape tomatoes

2 ears corn, shucked

Olive oil cooking spray, for misting

1 (12-ounce, or 340 g) bag tortilla chips

2 cups (225 g) shredded sharp Cheddar cheese

2 cups (225 g) shredded pepper Jack cheese

1 (15-ounce, or 425 g) can black beans, rinsed and drained

1 avocado, pitted and cut into small dice

3 scallions, white and green parts, thinly sliced

½ cup (8 g) chopped fresh cilantro

Sour cream, for garnishing

At least one day before you plan to make the nachos, make the pickled jalapeños (page 172).

Prepare a medium-hot single-level fire in a charcoal grill (see page 13) with a grill grate over the coals.

Thread the tomatoes onto skewers. Lightly mist the tomatoes and corn with cooking spray, place them on the grate, and close the grill lid. Grill until the tomatoes are softened and slightly blistered, about 5 minutes, and the corn is charred all over and tender, about 15 minutes, turning occasionally. Transfer to a cutting board. Remove the tomatoes from the skewers and cut the kernels off the corn.

Assemble the nachos on a half sheet pan. Start by spreading the tortilla chips evenly across the pan. Follow by sprinkling half each of the Cheddar, pepper Jack, tomatoes, corn, beans, avocado, pickled jalapeños, and scallions over the chips. Repeat the layers again with the remaining toppings.

Place the sheet pan on the grate and close the grill lid. Grill for about 5 minutes, until the cheeses are melted.

Scatter the cilantro over the nachos and dot with sour cream before serving.

HOT TIP

I like to use the most battered and blackened sheet pan from my kitchen on the grill so I don't have to worry about ruining it aesthetically, but you may wish to wrap your sheet pan in heavy-duty aluminum foil. It also helps make cleanup quicker!

PICKLED JALAPEÑOS

Pickled jalapeños often find their way into many other recipes besides nachos—from eggs and toast at breakfast to steak and baked potatoes at dinner. They can be as mild or as hot as you like, so don't be afraid to try a jar!

MAKES 1½ CUPS (135 G) PICKLED PEPPERS

½ cup (120 ml) distilled white vinegar

½ cup (120 ml) water

2 tablespoons (25 g) sugar

1 tablespoon (18 g) kosher salt

1 garlic clove, thinly sliced

½ teaspoon dried oregano

1½ cups (135 g) sliced jalapeño peppers

In a small saucepan over medium-high heat, combine the vinegar, water, sugar, salt, garlic, and oregano. Bring the brine to a simmer and stir until the sugar and salt dissolve. Remove from the heat.

Pack a pint-size (480 ml) jar with the jalapeños. Pour in the brine to fill the jar. Using a spoon, tamp down on the jalapeños to submerge them in the brine. Gently run a knife around the inside edge of the jar to release any trapped air bubbles. Seal the jar with a lid and refrigerate overnight to allow the flavors to develop. The pickled jalapeños will keep, refrigerated, for up to 3 months.

HOT TIP

If you want to cut down on heat, use 3 tablespoons (37.5 g) of sugar in the brine for sweeter pickles.

GRILLED CORN WITH SWEET CHILI-SOY GLAZE

In my opinion, no summer barbecue is complete without a pile of piping-hot fresh corn right off the grill. I like mine shucked before they hit the grate; the fire concentrates the sugars in the kernels, making them sweeter, at the same time adding a smoky char quintessential to grilling. Here, I intensify those natural flavors with an Asian-inspired glaze that's sweet, savory, and flecked with a little heat.

MAKES 6 SERVINGS

2 tablespoons (30 ml) soy sauce

2 tablespoons (40 g) sweet chili sauce

6 ears corn, shucked

Olive oil cooking spray, for misting

Butter, for serving (optional)

Prepare a medium-hot single-level fire in a charcoal grill (see page 13) with a grill grate over the coals.

In a small bowl, stir together the soy sauce and sweet chili sauce. Set aside until needed.

Mist the corn with cooking spray, arrange the ears on the grate, and close the grill lid. Grill for 5 to 10 minutes, turning occasionally, until the corn begins to char. Brush the glaze on the corn and continue grilling, with the lid closed, until the kernels are tender and charred all over, about 10 minutes, turning every 3 minutes and brushing with more glaze.

Serve with another slather of glaze on the corn and a swipe of butter, if desired.

GRILLED OYSTERS WITH KIMCHI BUTTER

Raw oysters usually get all the attention, but I'm partial to oysters on the grill. I love how the high heat softens the oyster flavor (making this method a great introduction for oyster-eating novices) and how the deep cups can hold a delicious sauce that blends beautifully with the oyster liquor. (Be sure to save the liquid inside the oysters when shucking!)

In this recipe I use a kimchi compound butter to enhance their briny flavor. The butter drips a bit into the flames while the oysters cook, adding a smoky, singed note to the sauce. Try not to leave the oysters on the grill too long—it's better to err on the side of undercooking to keep the meat tender.

MAKES 4 SERVINGS

Rock salt, for serving

8 tablespoons (1 stick, or 112 g) butter, at room temperature

⅓ cup (50 g) finely chopped Easy Homemade Kimchi (page 176) or store-bought kimchi

1 tablespoon (15 ml) kimchi liquid

16 oysters, cleaned (see page 182) and shucked

Minced fresh chives, for garnishing

Prepare a medium-hot single-level fire in a charcoal grill (see page 13) with a grill grate over the coals. Line a serving platter with rock salt for nestling the finished oysters.

In a small bowl, using a fork, mash and stir the butter, kimchi, and kimchi liquid until well incorporated. Spoon about 2 teaspoons of kimchi butter over each oyster. (Any unused butter can be refrigerated for future use. Try it on steaks, lobster, or other seafood, or over grilled vegetables and roasted potatoes.)

Arrange the oysters on the grate and close the grill lid. Grill for about 3 minutes, until the liquid is bubbling around the edges and the butter is fully melted. Transfer the oysters to your prepared serving platter, being careful not to spill any of the juices. Sprinkle the chives on top before serving.

> **HOT TIP**
>
> Rock salt is not the only ingredient you can use for serving oysters. Present them on mounds of uncooked rice, barley, lentils, or other grains and legumes, or nestle the oysters into beds of seaweed, leafy greens, or crumpled parchment paper to hold them upright.

EASY HOMEMADE KIMCHI

2 to 2½ pounds (908 g to 1.1 kg) Napa cabbage, quartered lengthwise, cored, and chopped into 1-inch (2.5 cm) pieces

¼ cup (72 g) kosher salt

¾ cup (75 g) julienned daikon

¾ cup (65 g) julienned carrot

¾ cup (169 g) thinly sliced leek, white and light green parts

3 scallions, white and green parts, cut into 1-inch (2.5 cm) segments

½ apple, cored and coarsely chopped

1 cup (240 ml) water

½ to ¾ cup (120 to 180 g) gochugaru (Korean red pepper powder; see recipe note)

¼ cup (60 ml) fish sauce

¼ cup (40 g) finely chopped yellow onion

¼ cup (40 g) finely chopped garlic

2 teaspoons minced peeled fresh ginger

If this is your first time fermenting, fear not! Basic homemade kimchi doesn't require any special equipment or tools, and, in fact, I always prefer to make smaller batches in Mason jars because they're easier to manage and store. The important thing to remember is that kimchi is a living, breathing product, so it needs time for the beneficial bacteria to flourish and for the flavors to develop. If your kimchi seems too pungent at first, let it sit for another day or so while it "ripens." Try to source the highest quality organic produce you can find for your fermentation, as fresh cabbage is essential for producing the natural liquid your brine needs.

MAKES 2 QUARTS (1.2 KG)

Place the cabbage into a large bowl and sprinkle it with the salt. Fill the bowl with cold water. Using your clean hands, stir the cabbage to distribute the salt evenly. Let sit for 1½ to 2 hours to let the cabbage expel moisture. Stir it with your hands and massage the leaves every 30 minutes to help release more liquid.

In a large colander, strain the cabbage and rinse it under cold running water to remove excess salt, constantly turning the leaves with your hands. The leaves should be soft and limp, and the volume reduced by half. Return the cabbage to the bowl.

Add the daikon, carrot, leek, and scallions to the bowl. Set aside.

In a blender, combine the apple, water, gochugaru (using up to the full amount if you prefer more heat), fish sauce, onion, garlic, and ginger. Purée until well blended. Pour the sauce over the vegetables and toss to coat. (If using your hands for this task, wear gloves to avoid getting the fiery red pepper sauce on your skin.)

RECIPE CONTINUES

Transfer the kimchi and all the sauce to two quart-size (960 ml) jars with lids, leaving 1 to 2 inches (2.5 to 5 cm) of space at the top to allow room for the vegetables to expand. Using a spoon, tamp down on the kimchi to help release more liquid from the vegetables and keep them submerged in the sauce. (Don't worry if it looks like there isn't enough liquid in the jars; as the vegetables ferment, they'll continue to release more liquid. Just remember to tamp down on the vegetables each day to push the liquid out and help them stay submerged.)

Loosely cover the jars with lids (don't tighten them too much, as the fermentation gases need space to escape) and place them in a baking dish to catch any overflow of liquid. Let sit at room temperature, away from direct sunlight, for at least 3 days. You'll start to see small bubbles in the jars, which are a sign the vegetables are fermenting properly.

On the third day, use a clean utensil to taste the kimchi from one of the jars. If it has a pleasantly tangy taste (due to beneficial bacteria brewing in your kimchi) and the flavors are balanced (not too salty and not too pungent), the jars are ready to be refrigerated. If not, let the jars sit for another 1 or 2 days and taste again.

A lower room temperature may slow the fermentation rate, so if your home tends to stay on the cooler side, it may take a few extra days to reach optimal flavor. On the flip side, a very warm house may speed fermentation, so start tasting your kimchi on the second day. Refrigerate it as soon as the flavor develops to your liking. Good, fresh kimchi should be crisp, tingly, and lightly acidic with a deep umami flavor. It should never have a rotten or "off" smell.

Refrigerated kimchi will continue to ferment, but at a much slower rate. It will keep for 3 to 4 months, refrigerated, after which the texture will start to decline and the flavor will turn more sour (though it never actually spoils, because it's fermented).

GRILLED LOBSTER TAILS WITH LEMONY HERB BUTTER

Grilled lobster tail sounds like an expensive and extravagant feast to pull off, but therein lies the benefit of grilling at home: you can have a luxe meal for much less than you'd spend eating out. And in my family, we almost always prefer going outside for our food, rather than just going out, because of this! The flavor you get from the luscious lemon-herb compound butter rivals (and perhaps surpasses) one you'd be served in a restaurant.

MAKES 4 SERVINGS

FOR THE HERB BUTTER

8 tablespoons (1 stick, or 112 g) butter, at room temperature

¼ cup (weight varies) minced fresh herbs

2 tablespoons (20 g) minced garlic

1 teaspoon lemon zest

1 teaspoon fresh lemon juice

FOR THE LOBSTERS

4 (8-ounce, or 225 g) lobster tails

Olive oil cooking spray, for misting

Kosher salt

Ground black pepper

Lemon wedges, for serving

Prepare a medium single-level fire in a charcoal grill (see page 13) with a grill grate over the coals.

To make the herb butter: In a small bowl, using a fork, mash and stir the butter, herbs, garlic, lemon zest, and lemon juice until well combined. Set aside until needed.

To butterfly the lobster tails:

1. Place each lobster tail, shell-side up, on a cutting board. Using heavy-duty kitchen shears, line up the bottom blade right under the shell and cut lengthwise down the center, stopping at the base of the tail. (The tail fin should remain intact.)
2. With a knife, cut along the same line to split the meat, stopping just before you slice all the way through to the bottom.
3. Turn the lobster tail over and snip the horizontal spines down the middle of the tail with your shears. If there are little fin-like legs (swimmerets) attached, snip those off and discard them.
4. Turn the lobster tail over again and pry it open like a book to separate and expose the meat.

Mist the meat with cooking spray and season with salt and pepper. Arrange the lobster tails, meat-side down, on the grate and close the grill lid. Grill for 5 to 7 minutes, until lightly charred.

Flip the lobsters onto their shells and brush the flesh generously with the compound butter, using about 2 tablespoons (28 g) per lobster. Close the grill lid and grill for about 5 minutes, until the flesh is opaque and firm to the touch and an instant-read thermometer inserted into the lobster registers 135°F (57°C). Serve the lobster tails with lemon wedges on the side.

GRILLED CLAMS IN TERIYAKI BUTTER

If you're feeding a crowd and clams are on the menu, this is my favorite way to get it done—and it can't get much easier than lighting a grill and throwing dozens of clams over the fire (a method that also makes for quite an impressive display). As soon as the clams open, take them off the grill (saving as much of the juices as possible) and drop them into a bowl to bathe in butter. The briny juices meld wonderfully with the sweet and savory teriyaki sauce to make a dipping broth you might be tempted to drink straight out of the bowl.

MAKES 4 SERVINGS

1 tablespoon (15 ml) soy sauce

1 tablespoon (15 ml) sake

1 tablespoon (15 ml) mirin

1 teaspoon sugar

8 tablespoons (1 stick, or 112 g) butter, cut into small cubes

2 pounds (908 g) littleneck clams, cleaned (see sidebar on page 182)

1 scallion, white and green parts, thinly sliced

Lemon wedges, for serving

Crusty bread, for serving

Prepare a medium-hot single-level fire in a charcoal grill (see page 13) with a grill grate over the coals.

On the stovetop, in a small saucepan over medium heat, combine the soy sauce, sake, mirin, and sugar. Stir until the sugar dissolves. Bring the mixture to a simmer and stir in the butter. Continue simmering, stirring frequently, until the butter melts and the sauce is well blended. Remove from the heat and set aside until needed.

Arrange the clams on the grate and close the grill lid. Grill for 4 to 6 minutes, until the clams begin to open. As soon as each clam opens, transfer it to a large bowl. Discard any clams that do not open after 8 minutes.

Drizzle the clams with the teriyaki butter sauce and sprinkle the scallion on top. Serve with lemon wedges and crusty bread to soak up all the delicious sauce.

HOW TO DE-GRIT CLAMS

By their very nature, clams sit buried in the sand, so it's inevitable they swallow sand and grit—sand and grit that can get into your food if you don't take the time to de-grit them before cooking. Also called purging, it's part of the overall process of cleaning clams. All you need is sea salt and water.

You see, clams aren't very smart. By dropping them into a brine, they'll think they're back in the ocean and do what clams do—swallow water and spit out sediment. When you harvest your own clams, you can actually purge them in the seawater you collected them from. But when you buy clams from the store, you have to purge them in a homemade solution that mimics the salinity of the ocean (which averages 3.5 percent). That means you need 35 grams of salt (about 2 table-spoons) per 1 liter (34 fluid ounces) of water.

To purge clams: In a large baking dish, combine 2 tablespoons (35 g) sea salt in 4 cups (960 ml) cold water. Stir to dissolve the salt. Scrub the clams with a stiff-bristle brush under cold running water to remove excess grit on the shells. Arrange them in the baking dish in a single layer. They should be completely covered in brine. (If not, make more using the same salt-to-wa-ter ratio.) Refrigerate the clams and let sit for 2 hours (or at least 1 hour if you're in a hurry) to purge themselves. Lift the clams out of the water, leaving all the sediment in the bottom of the dish. Give them a final rinse under cold running water before cooking.

You can also purge oysters (page 175) using this same technique.

EMPTY BEER CAN CHICKEN

So, why do I call this empty *beer can chicken? Contrary to popular belief, stuffing a can full of beer up a chicken's butt is just a waste of good beer. Real flavor comes from the smoky aroma inside a grill and the seasoning you use on the outside of the chicken—not from any fancy craft beer you sacrifice to the grill. Juicy meat comes from proper roasting technique, not from beer magically bubbling out of a can and steaming the chicken.*

What beer can chicken does get right, however, is utilizing a method called vertical roasting. Vertical roasting helps the meat heat more evenly because the legs (being closer to the coals) cook faster than the breasts, so the whole bird can be taken off the grill without being over- or undercooked. It also results in crisp, crackly skin, as the upright orientation drains fat well.

So save that beer (or whatever cold beverage you like to imbibe) for drinking, and, once you're done with it, repurpose it as a cheap and efficient roasting stand on the grill.

MAKES 4 SERVINGS

1 (12-ounce, or 360 ml) can of your favorite beverage

FOR THE SPICE RUB

3 tablespoons (45 g) packed light brown sugar

2 tablespoons (36 g) kosher salt

1 tablespoon (8 g) smoked paprika

1 tablespoon (8 g) sweet paprika

1 tablespoon (5 g) cayenne pepper

FOR THE CHICKEN

1 (4-pound, or 1.8 kg) whole chicken, giblets removed

Prepare a medium three-zone fire in a charcoal grill (see page 14) with a drip pan placed between the coals and a grill grate over the coals.

While you work, enjoy a can of your favorite beverage until empty and set aside.

To make the spice rub: In a small bowl, stir together all the rub ingredients. Set aside until ready to use. The spice rub can be stored in an airtight container in a cool, dark, dry place for up to 6 months (after which it starts to lose potency).

To make the chicken: Pat the chicken dry with paper towels. Liberally season the chicken all over with the spice rub (store any unused spice rub for future use).

Insert the empty can into the chicken's cavity and tuck the wings close to the body. Place the chicken on the grate over indirect heat, above the drip pan. Balance the chicken carefully on the can so the can and the two legs act as a tripod to keep it stable and upright. Close the grill lid.

RECIPE CONTINUES

Roast the chicken for 45 to 60 minutes (depending on the heat of your grill), until the skin is crisp and brown and an instant-read thermometer inserted into the chicken registers 160°F (71°C) in the breast (closest to the ribs without touching bone). If needed, add a few unlit pieces of charcoal about 20 minutes into roasting to maintain consistent heat.

Transfer the chicken to a cutting board and let rest for 10 minutes before carving. Serve the chicken with the pan drippings.

KOREAN GRILLED CHICKEN

Looking to try something new? A sweet, savory, and spicy Korean marinade adds a nice kick to everyday grilled chicken, and tastes like it took a lot more work than it actually did. Though it may sound like a special-occasion meal, Korean grilled chicken is a weeknight staple you can turn to when you don't have any dinner plans. Just freeze the chicken in its marinade and thaw in the morning before you leave for work. It's worth making and freezing a few batches to bail you out on those busy days!

MAKES 4 SERVINGS

½ cup (120 ml) soy sauce

½ cup (135 g) gochujang (Korean red pepper paste; see recipe note)

¼ cup (60 ml) toasted sesame oil

2 tablespoons (30 ml) rice vinegar

2 tablespoons (40 g) honey

2 tablespoons (30 g) packed light brown sugar

4 scallions, white and green parts, thinly sliced

6 garlic cloves, minced

2 pounds (908 g) bone-in skin-on chicken thighs

2 pounds (908 g) chicken drumsticks

Toasted sesame seeds, for garnishing

RECIPE NOTE

Gochujang is a fermented red pepper paste often sold in red plastic tubs; it's an essential ingredient in Korean recipes. It can be found in Korean markets, many specialty markets, and better supermarkets with an Asian food aisle, or online.

In a small bowl, whisk the soy sauce, gochujang, sesame oil, vinegar, honey, brown sugar, scallions, and garlic until combined.

As an optional step, cut a couple of shallow slits in each chicken thigh and drumstick to help the marinade penetrate more deeply. Place the chicken in a large resealable plastic bag and pour in the marinade. Seal the bag, shake to coat the chicken, and refrigerate for at least 2 hours or overnight. (I like to flip the bag at least once to redistribute the marinade.)

Prepare a medium-hot two-zone fire in a charcoal grill (see page 13) with a grill grate over the coals.

Remove the chicken from the marinade and arrange it, skin-side down, on the grate over direct heat. Discard the marinade. Grill the drumsticks for 5 to 8 minutes, turning occasionally, until deep brown all over. Grill the thighs, undisturbed, for 3 to 5 minutes, until the skin is brown and crispy. Move all the chicken pieces to indirect heat and close the grill lid. Grill the chicken, turning every 3 minutes, until an instant-read thermometer inserted into the thickest part of the meat reads 180°F to 185°F (82°C to 85°C). Transfer the chicken to a sheet pan.

Sprinkle a handful of sesame seeds over the chicken before serving.

HOT TIP

While chicken is technically safe to eat when it reaches 165°F (74°C), chicken thighs and drumsticks benefit from a longer cooking time, as the higher temperature helps break down connective tissue, rendering the meat more tender. This is why I always prefer dark meat on the grill, or tend to utilize a method like vertical roasting (see page 165) or spatchcocking (see page 183) to get the silkiest texture from the thighs without drying out the breasts.

ARTICHOKE, SUN-DRIED TOMATO, AND FETA-STUFFED FLANK STEAK

I'm always thrilled when a recipe can transform an inexpensive item into an incredible meal. In this case, I take a cheap cut of meat—lean, fibrous flank steak, which is rather ordinary on its own—and stuff it with scrumptious Mediterranean ingredients that stand up to the smoky grill. Slice the steak into pinwheels before serving and you have an impressive presentation worthy of company, or just a special dinner for you.

MAKES 4 TO 6 SERVINGS

1 (14-ounce, or 395 g) can quartered artichoke hearts, drained

½ cup (57.5 g) oil-packed sun-dried tomatoes, drained

1 shallot, coarsely chopped

¼ cup (9 g) packed fresh basil

2 tablespoons (30 ml) olive oil

2 tablespoons (30 ml) red wine vinegar

2 garlic cloves, peeled

½ teaspoon kosher salt, plus more for seasoning

¼ teaspoon ground black pepper, plus more for seasoning

⅓ cup (50 g) crumbled feta cheese

1 (2- to 2½-pound, or 908 g to 1.1 kg) flank steak, butterflied and trimmed of excess fat

Prepare a medium-hot two-zone fire in a charcoal grill (see page 13) with a grill grate over the coals.

In a food processor, combine the artichoke hearts, sun-dried tomatoes, shallot, basil, olive oil, vinegar, garlic, salt, and pepper. Pulse until very finely chopped, scraping down the sides of the bowl with a rubber spatula every so often to incorporate them. Add the feta and pulse to combine. The filling should be well blended but still a little chunky. Set aside.

Place the butterflied steak on a cutting board. The meat should be about ¼ inch (0.6 cm) thick; if it's thicker in certain parts, pound it flat with a meat mallet or rolling pin for even thickness.

Season the steak on both sides with salt and pepper. Spread the filling evenly on the steak, leaving about a 1-inch (2.5 cm) border all around. (You might not need to use all the filling.) Starting at the edge closest to you, roll the steak firmly (up and away from you), being careful not to squeeze the filling out the sides. Tie the steak roll every 1½ to 2 inches (3.5 to 5 cm) with kitchen twine to secure.

Place the steak on the grate over direct heat. Grill, undisturbed, for 3 minutes per side until browned, 12 minutes total. Move the steak over indirect heat and close the grill lid. Continue grilling for about 15 minutes more, until an instant-read thermometer inserted in the center of the steak reads 125°F (52°C) for medium-rare.

Transfer the steak to a cutting board and let rest for 10 minutes. Cut the steak into 1-inch (2.5 cm) slices and remove the twine before serving.

BOURBON AND PECAN GRILL-BAKED APPLES

There's something about this recipe—between the sweet, ripe apples and the traditional blend of sugar and spice—that feels like home to me. It's warm and familiar, simple and timeless, and doesn't need much more than a fork to eat it. That's not to say you shouldn't (and you definitely should) eat it with a scoop of ice cream—after all, dessert is meant to be indulgent.

MAKES 4 TO 8 SERVINGS

4 baking apples, such as Honeycrisp, Fuji, or Pink Lady

4 tablespoons (56 g) butter, at room temperature

½ cup (120 g) packed light brown sugar

½ cup (55 g) chopped pecans

¾ teaspoon ground cinnamon

8 teaspoons (40 ml) bourbon

Prepare a medium two-zone fire in a charcoal grill (see page 13) with a grill grate over the coals.

With a paring knife, cut out the core from the top of each apple to create a large deep hollow, being careful not to cut all the way through to the bottom.

In a small bowl, stir together the butter, brown sugar, pecans, and cinnamon. Stuff each apple with an equal amount of the butter mixture and make a small well with a spoon in the stuffing. Slowly pour 2 teaspoons bourbon into the well of each apple.

Arrange the apples upright on the grate over indirect heat and close the grill lid. Bake for 20 to 25 minutes, until the sugar is caramelized and the apples are tender.

To serve, slice each apple in half or in quarters lengthwise.

CHAPTER 7

FEASTING ... WITH SMOKE

Rooted in Native American history, plank grilling originated from Pacific Northwest tribes cooking their salmon on cedar slabs over an open flame. While salmon is still commonly associated with this method, modern-day planking gives us many more options for the grill—from fruits and vegetables to pizza and meatloaf.

What makes it so special is that a plank of wood is more than just a pretty platter. Planks infuse the food with a sweet, smoky aroma, adding depth to even the blandest ingredients. Flavorful juices don't drip off into the fire, so food stays rich and succulent. Small or delicate foods won't fall apart or slip through the grate. And, for the newly initiated, planks are also forgiving; you can leave (forget?) the food for a few extra minutes and it will still be waiting for you.

CHOOSING A PLANK

When choosing a plank for your grill, you have to consider two things: size and type of wood.

Most grilling planks are ⅜ to ½ inch (0.9 to 1 cm) thick and measure 12 x 7 inches (30 x 18 cm). This is the minimum size you'll need for all the planking recipes in this book. Some grilling planks also come in squares, ovals, and individual serving sizes, so you can match plank to food for both practicality and presentation.

> **HOT TIP**
>
> Check your local lumberyard for inexpensive—and, most importantly, untreated—hardwood planks you can cut down to size.

The most common plank wood is Western red cedar. If you're only going to get one type of wood, you can't go wrong with cedar; if you're open to experimentation, stock a variety of grilling planks in your outdoor kitchen and discover how each type of wood infuses your food with its own distinct aroma.

Western red cedar has a strong, spicy, and smoky sweet flavor that works well with fish, seafood, vegetables, fruits, and soft cheeses.

Hickory has a heavy, intense flavor that pairs perfectly with beef, lamb, wild game, and bacon.

Oak falls in the middle of the spectrum with its bold, but not overpowering, flavor. It complements a wide range of foods, including beef, chicken, pork, and fish.

Cherry is a fruity, smoky wood whose sweetness pairs well with chicken, turkey, lamb, and duck.

Maple is a subtly sweet wood with a balanced flavor, so it goes well with many foods, such as pork, chicken, turkey, vegetables, fruits, and cheeses.

Alder has a mild, earthy, and slightly nutty flavor that complements white fish, seafood, vegetables, and fruits.

Preparing the Plank for Grilling

Step 1: Soaking: Start by soaking the plank in water for at least 1 hour (or overnight). If you're feeling creative, you can soak the plank in beer, white wine, apple juice, or other liquids for a little extra flavor.

This important step not only keeps the plank from catching fire and over-charring, but it also helps the plank last longer, so you can reuse it. I like to soak my planks in a baking dish with a heavy pot to weight them down, and I usually flip them halfway through to ensure they're thoroughly soaked.

> **HOT TIP**
>
> If you often forget to soak planks before you want to grill, soak them ahead of time. Wrap the soaked planks in plastic bags and store them in the freezer. The frozen planks can be preheated on the grill without thawing (just allow a few extra minutes for the wood to start smoking).

Step 2: Preheating: Preheating the plank serves two purposes: to control warping (as most woods, with the exception of cedar, tend to warp when placed over heat) and impart a deeper wood flavor to the food.

Begin by firing up your charcoal grill. Arrange the coals into a two-zone fire (see page 13) with a grill grate over the coals. Place the soaked plank on the grate over direct heat and close the grill lid. Let it preheat for about 5 minutes. When you see wisps of light gray smoke emanating from the grill, open the lid and check the plank. If it hasn't bowed, you can start grilling. If it's warped, using tongs, flip the plank over and close the lid again. Let it heat for a couple more minutes until it flattens out.

Grilling with the Plank

Once the plank is preheated, using tongs, flip it over and move it over indirect heat. Place your food on the scorched side of the plank and close the grill lid. Grill as directed in the recipe instructions. Adjust the dampers as needed to maintain a consistent temperature and light gray smoke (see page 159 for more on using the grill's dampers).

To remove the plank from the grill, firmly grip the edge closest to you with tongs and slide the plank onto a sheet pan. Remember, the plank will be very hot, as will the bottom of the sheet pan when you carry it to the table. The food can be served on the plank or plated individually for guests.

Cleaning and Storing the Plank

As you do with dishes, soak the plank in water to loosen any food remnants. Scrub it with soap and water and rinse well to remove any soap residue. Let the plank air-dry completely to prevent molding before storing.

A used plank can be cleaned, dried, soaked, and reused two to four times before it becomes too blackened. Alternate the sides you preheat each time so the wood chars more evenly, prolonging the plank's usability. Try to reuse the same plank to grill the same types of food, particularly fish and seafood. Once the plank has reached the end of its life, you can break it apart with a hammer and use it as smoking wood.

PLANKED FIGS WITH PROSCIUTTO AND GOAT CHEESE

The aroma of ripe fresh seasonal figs shines in this recipe, because the supple fruit just drinks up all that delicious wood smoke from the plank. Each little nugget is a pure flavor bomb with a harmony of sweet, savory, and smoky. I like the light and subtle sweetness of maple here, but cedar will give an almost spicy edge that pairs well with the prosciutto. You can serve these figs as finger food, or make a little more dressing to turn them into a salad.

MAKES 6 SERVINGS

1 tablespoon (20 g) honey

1 tablespoon (15 ml) balsamic vinegar

6 fresh figs

2 tablespoons (18 g) crumbled goat cheese

3 thin slices prosciutto, halved lengthwise

Ground black pepper

Baby arugula, for serving (optional)

Soak a maple or cedar plank in water for at least 1 hour before you plan to grill.

In a small bowl, whisk the honey and vinegar until well blended. Set aside until needed.

Prepare a medium-hot two-zone fire in a charcoal grill (see page 13) with a grill grate over the coals.

Cut an X-shaped slit in the top of a fig, slicing through about halfway down. Pull the fig apart slightly and put 1 teaspoon of goat cheese inside. Wrap the fig with a slice of prosciutto, secure with a toothpick, and sprinkle with a pinch of pepper. Repeat the process for the remaining figs.

Preheat the plank until it starts to smoke (see page 194). Turn the plank over and move it to indirect heat. Arrange the figs, stems up, on the plank and close the grill lid. Roast for about 15 minutes, until the figs are softened and scorched at the tips and the prosciutto is browned and crisp on the edges.

Drizzle the figs with the dressing before serving.

For a more substantial first course, divide the arugula between two or three plates and nestle the figs on each bed of greens.

PLANKED PEARS WITH GORGONZOLA AND HONEY

If I'm already making dinner on the grill, I usually make dessert on the grill, too. Grilled fruit (or in this case, grill-roasted fruit) takes the agony out of deciding what to serve when the last of the plates have been scraped off and your guests are settling into a long night of storytelling.

It's simple: a platter of sweet, caramelized pears, sharpened with creamy Gorgonzola, and washed down with your favorite digestif.

MAKES 4 SERVINGS

1 tablespoon (14 g) butter, at room temperature

1 tablespoon (20 g) honey

2 pears, halved lengthwise and cored (see recipe note)

¼ cup (30 g) crumbled Gorgonzola cheese

Soak a cedar plank in water for at least 1 hour before you plan to grill.

Prepare a medium-hot two-zone fire in a charcoal grill (see page 13) with a grill grate over the coals.

In a small bowl, stir together the butter and honey until well blended. Brush the cut sides of the pears generously with the butter mixture and sprinkle the Gorgonzola on top.

Preheat the plank until it starts to smoke (see page 194). Turn the plank over and move it to indirect heat. Arrange the pears on the plank and close the grill lid. Roast for about 25 minutes, until the pears are tender and scorched around the edges.

RECIPE NOTE
I like Anjou or Bosc pears because they hold their shape and texture well on the grill, but you can use any firm-fleshed variety.

PLANK-ROASTED SUMMER VEGETABLE SKEWERS WITH SPICY CILANTRO SAUCE

No backyard cookout is complete without a heaping platter of grilled vegetables, and, because they're basically a blank canvas for flavor experimentation, I like to pair them with bold, bright sauces that turn them into something more than just a side dish. One such sauce is based on the fiery Yemenite condiment called zhoug. The spice might be the first thing you notice when you taste it, but zhoug is much more complex, with a layer of warm, fragrant spices balancing the freshness of the cilantro and the heat of the peppers.

Zhoug is and should be spicy, but you can adjust the level of heat to your preference. I often use a combination of whatever peppers I currently have in the kitchen, including serrano peppers, Hungarian wax peppers, and Thai bird's-eye chiles. Each batch turns out a little different each time (even when I use the same peppers), but is always full of flavor and character. The sauce also gets better as it ages, so if it tastes too bitter or spicy right out of the food processor, let it sit for a few hours and it will mellow as the flavors develop more fully.

MAKES 4 SERVINGS

HOT TIP

The trick to getting evenly roasted vegetables is choosing (or cutting) them all roughly the same size, including the cherry tomatoes. I like using early summer produce, as the vegetables tend to be smaller and more tender.

FOR THE SAUCE

2 jalapeño peppers, coarsely chopped

2 Fresno chile peppers, coarsely chopped

4 garlic cloves, peeled

2 cups (32 g) packed fresh cilantro

½ cup (120 ml) olive oil

½ teaspoon ground cumin

½ teaspoon ground cardamom

¼ teaspoon kosher salt

FOR THE SKEWERS

8 ounces (225 g) Italian eggplant, cut into 1-inch (2.5 cm) chunks

8 ounces (225 g) zucchini, cut into 1-inch (2.5 cm) chunks

8 ounces (225 g) golden zucchini, cut into 1-inch (2.5 cm) chunks (see recipe note)

8 ounces (225 g) cherry tomatoes

Olive oil cooking spray, for misting

Kosher salt

Ground black pepper

RECIPE CONTINUES

RECIPE NOTE
In place of golden zucchini, you can use yellow straightneck squash, crookneck squash, or another summer squash.

Soak a cedar plank in water for at least 1 hour before you plan to grill.

Prepare a medium-hot two-zone fire in a charcoal grill (see page 13) with a grill grate over the coals.

To make the sauce: In a food processor, combine the jalapeños, Fresno peppers, and garlic. Pulse until finely chopped. Scrape down the sides of the bowl with a rubber spatula and add the cilantro. Pulse until all the ingredients are finely chopped and combined. Add the olive oil, cumin, cardamom, and salt. Process until smooth, scraping down the sides of the bowl as needed. Set aside until ready to serve.

To make the skewers: Thread the eggplant, zucchini, golden zucchini, and tomatoes onto skewers, alternating the vegetables on each skewer. Mist the vegetables with cooking spray and season with salt and pepper.

Preheat the plank until it starts to smoke (see page 194). Turn the plank over and move it to indirect heat. Arrange the skewers on the plank and close the grill lid. Roast for about 30 minutes, until the vegetables are tender to your liking. Serve the skewers with small bowls of cilantro sauce on the side for dipping.

SURPRISE! SEEDS ARE NOT THE SPICY PART

Contrary to popular belief—and far too many recipes telling you to remove the seeds if you want to tone down the spice—seeds are not the source of a chile pepper's heat. The plant's taste bud–tingling compounds, capsaicin, are actually contained in the ribs of the chile peppers. While the seeds may be coated in some of the capsaicin because they touch the ribs, they do not contain any heat. So, if you want to cut down on the fire, remove the fleshy membrane inside the pepper.

PLANK-ROASTED HASSELBACK POTATOES WITH AVOCADO AIOLI

How do you make something so satisfyingly good even better? Slice it up all fancy style, roast it on a plank, and serve it with a rich, creamy aioli that somehow makes everything feel light and fresh. Hasselback potatoes are the perfect way to roast potatoes if you love crisp, brown edges (like your favorite fries) but don't want to give up the soft, velvety middles (like mashed potatoes). Here, you get the best of both worlds!

MAKES 4 SERVINGS

FOR THE AIOLI

2 garlic cloves, peeled

1 avocado, halved and pitted

⅓ cup (75 g) mayonnaise

1 teaspoon fresh lemon juice

½ teaspoon kosher salt

¼ teaspoon ground black pepper

FOR THE POTATOES

4 (8-ounce, or 225 g) russet potatoes

4 garlic cloves, thinly sliced

¼ cup (20 g) shaved Parmesan cheese

Olive oil, for drizzling

Kosher salt

Ground black pepper

Melted butter, for serving

Soak a cedar plank in water for at least 1 hour before you plan to grill.

Prepare a medium-hot two-zone fire in a charcoal grill (see page 13) with a grill grate over the coals.

To make the aioli: In a food processor, pulse the garlic until finely chopped. Scrape down the sides of the bowl and add the avocado, mayonnaise, lemon juice, salt, and pepper. Process until smooth, scraping down the sides every so often to incorporate all the ingredients. Set aside until ready to serve.

To make the potatoes: If your potatoes do not sit flat without rolling, slice a ¼-inch (0.6 cm) piece off the bottoms to make them more stable. Cut even slits in each potato widthwise, spacing them about ¼ inch (0.6 cm) apart, stopping just before you cut through to the bottom. Rinse the potatoes under running water to remove any starch between the slices.

Tuck the garlic slices and Parmesan between each slice. Drizzle olive oil over the potatoes, making sure the oil gets in between some of the slices. Season with salt and pepper.

Preheat the plank until it starts to smoke (see page 194). Turn the plank over and move it over indirect heat. Arrange the potatoes on the plank and close the grill lid. Roast for about 1 hour, until the skin is browned and crispy and the flesh is moist and tender.

To serve, drizzle melted butter over the potatoes and offer the aioli for dipping.

HOT TIP

If you tend to have a heavy hand with a knife, place two chopsticks or wooden spoon handles along both lengths of the potato to help with slicing. The chopsticks will keep you from accidentally slicing all the way through the potato.

CEDAR-PLANKED TOMATOES STUFFED WITH MUSHROOMS AND GRUYÈRE

By their nature, stuffed tomatoes aren't grand—they're comfort food. They're made at home, served with a simple scoop of rice, and you'll rarely find them on a menu at your local French or Vietnamese restaurant.

Tomates farcies, as they're called in French, were a staple of my childhood. Though my family's version leans traditional Vietnamese, I've always liked to tinker with the ingredients to make peak-season tomatoes really shine. This is one of my favorite versions and a good use for tomatoes "on the vine" at the market, as the green stems make lovely little handles on the "hats" for serving.

MAKES 4 SERVINGS

8 ripe but firm tomatoes (about 4 ounces, or 115 g each, or 2 pounds, or 908 g total), preferably with stems attached

½ cup (25 g) fine fresh bread crumbs, from day-old bread

½ cup (60 g) grated Gruyère cheese, plus more for sprinkling

½ cup (35 g) finely chopped cremini mushrooms

½ cup (80 g) minced shallot

2 tablespoons (8 g) minced fresh parsley

2 tablespoons (5 g) minced fresh basil

2 garlic cloves, minced

1 teaspoon minced fresh thyme

½ teaspoon kosher salt

¼ teaspoon ground black pepper

2 tablespoons (30 ml) olive oil, plus more for drizzling

Soak a cedar plank in water for at least 1 hour before you plan to grill.

Prepare a medium-hot two-zone fire in a charcoal grill (see page 13) with a grill grate over the coals.

Using a paring knife, cut off the top ½ inch (1 cm) from each tomato, reserving the top, and cut out the core. Using a spoon, scoop out the innards, leaving a ½-inch (1 cm)-thick shell. Save the juices, seeds, and flesh to make the marinara sauce on page 188, or discard. Arrange the tomatoes (with their accompanying tops) on a sheet pan and set aside.

In a medium bowl, stir together the bread crumbs, Gruyère, mushrooms, shallot, parsley, basil, garlic, thyme, salt, pepper, and olive oil. Stuff each tomato with 3 to 4 tablespoons (18 to 24 g) of the bread crumb mixture and top with a sprinkle of Gruyère. Place the tops back on the tomatoes, like little hats, and drizzle with olive oil.

Preheat the plank until it starts to smoke (see page 194). Turn the plank over and move it to indirect heat. Arrange the tomatoes on the plank and close the grill lid. Grill for about 30 minutes, until the tomatoes are soft, the filling is golden brown, and the cheese is melted.

2 tablespoons (30 ml) olive oil

1 shallot, minced

2 garlic cloves, minced

1 (28-ounce, or 790 g) can whole peeled tomatoes, undrained

1 tablespoon (4 g) minced fresh oregano

Pinch red pepper flakes

Kosher salt

FOR THE MEATBALLS

12 (about 1 pound, or 454 g) Italian-style meatballs

Kosher salt

Ground black pepper

Grated Parmesan cheese, for sprinkling

Cooked spaghetti, for serving (optional)

PLANKED MEATBALLS WITH MARINARA SAUCE

Part of being a good and efficient cook is knowing where to focus your efforts and where to take shortcuts—and this is especially true for these planked meatballs with marinara sauce. While I always prefer homemade meatballs, my butcher sells a fine selection of meatballs I'm happy to use on nights when I just want to get dinner done. The woodsy flavor from the plank makes any meatball that much better, and the homemade marinara (which comes together quickly and easily) beats any from a jar.

I like these meatballs on a bed of spaghetti with more sauce on top, but you can also layer them between slider buns with fresh basil, tuck them inside hoagie rolls with melted provolone, or spear them with toothpicks to serve as an appetizer.

MAKES 4 SERVINGS

Soak an oak plank in water for at least 1 hour before you plan to grill.

Prepare a medium-hot two-zone fire in a charcoal grill (see page 13) with a grill grate over the coals.

To make the marinara sauce: On the stovetop, heat a medium skillet over medium-high heat. Add the olive oil and shallot. Cook for 1 to 2 minutes, until the shallot is translucent. Stir in the garlic, tomatoes, oregano, and red pepper flakes and bring the sauce to a rapid simmer. Reduce the heat and keep the sauce at a slow, steady simmer, stirring occasionally and mashing the tomatoes with the back of a spoon as they break down. Cook for at least 30 minutes until ready to use. The longer the sauce simmers, the thicker and richer it becomes. Taste the sauce and add salt if needed. (If you prefer a smoother sauce, blend it before using.)

To make the meatballs: Season the meatballs with salt and pepper.

RECIPE CONTINUES

If you want to try your hand at homemade meatballs, follow my recipe for Bacon-Wrapped Meatloaf on a Plank (page 211)—omitting the bacon—and shape the mixture into 1½-inch (3.5 cm) balls. Cook as instructed above.

Preheat the plank until it starts to smoke (see page 194). Turn the plank over and move it to indirect heat. Arrange the meatballs on the plank and close the grill lid. Grill for about 10 minutes, until the meatballs are browned all over.

Spoon about 1 tablespoon (15 g) of marinara sauce over each meatball. (Reserve unused marinara for future use or to coat spaghetti for a full meal.) Close the grill lid and grill for about 5 minutes.

Sprinkle Parmesan over the meatballs and close the grill lid. Grill for 5 minutes more, until the cheese melts. An instant-read thermometer inserted into the center of the meatball should register 160°F (71°C). Serve with more Parmesan sprinkled on top and cooked spaghetti, if desired.

CEDAR-PLANKED HOT HAM AND BRIE MELTS

Ham and Brie on a plank is one of my favorite twists on the traditional grilled cheese. The cedar plank infuses the sandwiches with a subtle aroma that seems to enhance the earthiness of soft-ripened Brie. I like to finish them directly on the grill for a few minutes to add a little crispness and char to the bread.

MAKES 4 SERVINGS

8 slices country bread

Mayonnaise, for spreading

Dijon mustard, for spreading

8 to 12 ounces (225 to 340 g) deli ham, thinly sliced

1 (8-ounce, or 225 g) wheel Brie cheese, cut into ¼-inch (0.6 cm) slices (see recipe note)

Hot Pepper Jelly (page 210) or store-bought hot pepper jelly, for spreading

Soak a cedar plank in water for at least 1 hour before you plan to grill.

Prepare a medium-hot two-zone fire in a charcoal grill (see page 13) with a grill grate over the coals.

On 4 bread slices, spread a thin coat of mayonnaise on one side. Flip the bread and spread a thin coat of Dijon on the other side. Layer a few slices each of the ham and cheese on top.

On the remaining 4 bread slices, slather the jelly. Place them, jelly-side down, on the sandwich. Spread a thin coat of mayonnaise on top.

Preheat the plank until it starts to smoke (see page 194). Turn the plank over and move it over indirect heat. Arrange the sandwiches on the plank and close the grill lid. Grill for 10 to 12 minutes, until the cheese is melted and the bread is toasted. Remove the sandwiches from the plank and move them over to the direct heat side. Grill the sandwiches on the grate, uncovered, for about 1 minute per side, until good grill marks form.

RECIPE NOTE
The rind on Brie is edible, so no need to remove it before slicing.

HOT PEPPER JELLY

The sweet heat of this pepper jelly pairs beautifully with the creamy Brie and tangy mustard in my Cedar-Planked Hot Ham and Brie Melts (page 208), but you'll also love this on biscuits and crostini, glazed onto chicken or pork, or layered on other soft cheeses such as Camembert.

MAKES 3 (8-OUNCE, OR 225 G) JARS

2 cups (300 g) finely chopped bell peppers, any color or a mix

½ cup (120 ml) apple cider vinegar

1 teaspoon red pepper flakes

3 tablespoons (36 g) Sure-Jell Less or No Sugar Needed Premium Fruit Pectin

1 teaspoon butter

1½ cups (300 g) sugar

To prepare your jars and lids, place them in a large saucepan and cover with at least 1 inch (2.5 cm) of water. Heat them on the stovetop over medium heat and keep them warm while you make the jelly. (Alternatively, wash them in the dishwasher right before you begin so they'll remain warm after the heated drying cycle.)

In a wide heavy-bottomed saucepan over medium-high heat, combine the bell peppers, vinegar, and red pepper flakes. Stir in the pectin and butter. Bring the mixture to a full rolling boil (a vigorous boil that doesn't stop bubbling when stirred), stirring constantly. Stir in the sugar. Return the mixture to a full rolling boil and boil for 1 minute, stirring constantly. Remove the saucepan from the heat.

Drain the jars and place them on a clean kitchen towel. Ladle the hot jelly into the warm jars, filling to within ½ inch (1 cm) of the rims. Stir the jelly to redistribute the peppers (they have a tendency to float), and seal the jars with lids. Let them come to room temperature before refrigerating. The jelly should set overnight or within 24 hours. The jelly will keep, refrigerated, for up to 3 weeks.

HOT TIP

Make sure your red pepper flakes are fresh for the best flavor! You can also use any combination of peppers in this recipe to make the jelly as hot or mild as you prefer. In place of red pepper flakes, try a fresh hot chile, such as serrano or habanero (if you like a little kick), or a jalapeño for a tamer flavor.

BACON-WRAPPED MEATLOAF ON A PLANK

Meatloaf on the grill. It's every bit as amazing as you might imagine. At first thought, it doesn't sound like it could work from a logistical standpoint. But enter a grilling plank and—suddenly—you can use the fragrant smoke of the wood to your advantage.

There are endless variations on the classic Americana recipe, but these are a few of my favorite tricks for achieving a gorgeous, succulent, and tender meatloaf: sauté the vegetables first to enhance flavor and moisture; use a blend of freshly ground chuck and Italian sausage for extra richness; mix in rolled oats to retain all those delicious juices; and add bacon because . . . well, bacon. Your favorite barbecue sauce just sends it over the top!

MAKES 6 SERVINGS

2 tablespoons (28 g) butter

⅓ cup (53 g) minced onion

⅓ cup (37 g) minced carrot

⅓ cup (50 g) minced bell pepper, any color

2 garlic cloves, minced

6 thin bacon slices

2 large eggs, beaten

1 tablespoon (15 ml) Worcestershire sauce

1 tablespoon (6 g) ground black pepper

2 teaspoons kosher salt

1 teaspoon smoked paprika

½ cup (78 g) old-fashioned rolled oats (see recipe note on page 212)

½ cup (125 g) of your favorite barbecue sauce, plus more for glazing

1 pound (454 g) ground chuck

1 pound (454 g) bulk mild Italian sausage

Soak an oak or cedar plank in water for at least 1 hour before you plan to grill.

Prepare a medium-hot two-zone fire in a charcoal grill (see page 13) or, preferably if your grill is large enough, a three-zone fire (see page 14) with a grill grate over the coals.

On the stovetop, in a medium skillet over medium-high heat, melt the butter. Add the onion, carrot, and bell pepper. Stir to combine. Cook for 6 to 8 minutes, until the onion is translucent and the carrot has softened. Stir in the garlic. Cook for about 1 minute, until very fragrant. Remove from the heat and set aside.

Line a loaf pan with parchment paper. Drape the bacon in a crisscross pattern across the loaf pan and leave the ends hanging over the edge.

In a large bowl, combine the eggs, Worcestershire, pepper, salt, paprika, oats, barbecue sauce, and cooked vegetables. Add the ground chuck and Italian sausage. Work the ingredients together by hand until just combined (avoid overmixing).

RECIPE CONTINUES

HOT TIP

If you don't have a loaf pan, spoon the meatloaf mixture onto the preheated plank and pat it into a 9 x 5-inch (23 x 13 cm) loaf-shaped mound. Cut the bacon strips in half, drape them over the meatloaf, and grill, following the instructions as listed.

RECIPE NOTE

Instant (quick) oats can be substituted if that's what you have.

(At this stage, you can cook a spoonful of the mixture in a skillet to taste and adjust any seasonings, if desired. This is an optional step but helpful if you want to know how your barbecue sauce works with the recipe.)

Pat the meatloaf mixture into your prepared loaf pan and fold the bacon ends over the meatloaf.

Preheat the plank until it starts to smoke (see page 194). Put on a pair of heatproof gloves, turn the plank over, and place the toasted side on top of your loaf pan. Then, holding onto the plank and the pan so they're tight against each other, turn both over and place them on the indirect heat side of the grill. Carefully slide the pan off the meatloaf (using the parchment to help you, if necessary) and discard the parchment. Close the grill lid. Grill for about 30 minutes, until the bacon is crisp and brown on the edges and the meatloaf has formed a crust.

Brush the top of the meatloaf with more barbecue sauce and close the grill lid. Continue grilling for 20 to 30 minutes more, until an instant-read thermometer inserted into the center of the meatloaf reaches 155°F (68°C). (If you have a two-zone fire, rotate the plank 180 degrees at this halfway point for even cooking.)

Let the meatloaf rest for 10 minutes before slicing and serving.

PLANKED HALIBUT WITH ORANGE-MISO GLAZE

Thick and meaty, firm yet flaky, halibut has a heartier texture and flavor than most other white fish on the market. It's a bit more forgiving because it won't overcook as easily as thinner fillets, and it can handle a little more time on the grill, which means more time to infuse all that wonderfully smoky flavor. For all these reasons, I like to pair halibut with a cedar plank and a zippy orange-miso sauce flecked with ginger. As it cooks on the grill, the sauce turns into a shimmering glaze that stands up perfectly to the hefty fillet.

MAKES 4 SERVINGS

2 tablespoons (40 g) orange marmalade

2 tablespoons (34 g) white or yellow miso

1 teaspoon sesame oil

1 teaspoon soy sauce

1 teaspoon mirin

1 teaspoon grated peeled fresh ginger

4 (8-ounce, or 225 g) halibut fillets

Toasted sesame seeds, for garnishing

Finely chopped scallions, white and green parts, for garnishing

Soak a cedar plank in water for at least 1 hour before you plan to grill.

Prepare a medium-hot two-zone fire in a charcoal grill (see page 13) with a grill grate over the coals.

In a small bowl, whisk the marmalade, miso, sesame oil, soy sauce, mirin, and ginger until combined.

Thoroughly pat the halibut dry with paper towels and generously brush the fillets with the glaze.

Preheat the plank until it starts to smoke (see page 194). Turn the plank over and move it over indirect heat. Arrange the halibut on the plank and close the grill lid. Grill for 15 to 20 minutes, until an instant-read thermometer inserted into the thickest part of the flesh reaches 130°F to 135°F (54°C to 57°C). (Depending on the thickness of your fillets, cooking time may vary by a few minutes.)

Garnish with sesame seeds and scallions before serving.

PLANKED SHRIMP WITH SPANISH GREEN SAUCE

If you're serving shrimp on a plank, it has to be special. And this bright, tangy green sauce, inspired by the Canary Islands' mojo verde (Spanish for—you guessed it—green sauce) sends it over the top. I love to put this dish out as an eye-catching appetizer, but it also serves two to four people as a delicious—and splendidly different—option for surf-and-turf meals. The mojo verde can be drizzled over your steak and vegetables, or served with other seafood as well.

MAKES 4 SERVINGS

FOR THE SAUCE

2 cups (120 g) packed fresh parsley

2 garlic cloves, peeled

1 cup (240 ml) olive oil

2 tablespoons (30 ml) sherry vinegar

½ teaspoon kosher salt

½ teaspoon ground cumin

Pinch red pepper flakes

FOR THE SHRIMP

1 pound (454 g) large shrimp, peeled and deveined

Kosher salt

Ground black pepper

Soak a cedar plank in water for at least 1 hour before you plan to grill.

Prepare a medium two-zone fire in a charcoal grill (see page 13) with a grill grate over the coals.

To make the sauce: In a food processor, combine the parsley and garlic. Pulse until coarsely chopped. Scrape down the sides of the bowl with a rubber spatula and add the olive oil, vinegar, salt, cumin, and red pepper flakes. Process until smooth. Reserve 3 tablespoons (45 ml) of the sauce for glazing the shrimp and set aside the remaining sauce for serving.

To make the shrimp: Thoroughly pat the shrimp dry with paper towels and season both sides with salt and pepper. Brush the shrimp with the reserved sauce.

Preheat the plank until it starts to smoke (see page 194). Turn the plank over and move it over indirect heat. Arrange the shrimp on the plank and close the grill lid. Grill for about 5 minutes, until the flesh is opaque. Serve the shrimp with the remaining sauce for dipping.

CEDAR-PLANKED SALMON WITH SOY-GINGER GLAZE

Salmon and cedar planks go hand in hand when you think plank grilling. The technique keeps the delicate flesh from burning or tearing on the grate, and the fish picks up the smoky flavors from the grill while it gently steams. Here, cedar also plays nicely with the deep, warm flavors of a honey, soy, sesame glaze. Brush it on before the salmon goes on the grill and the fish just soaks up all those vivid flavors. Finish with more glaze spooned over the top— or, if you're like me, make a little extra to dress side dishes like grilled baby bok choy or steamed rice.

MAKES 4 SERVINGS

¼ cup (85 g) honey

2 tablespoons (30 ml) soy sauce

1 tablespoon (15 ml) toasted sesame oil

1 tablespoon (15 ml) rice vinegar

1 tablespoon (8 g) grated peeled fresh ginger

2 garlic cloves, minced

4 (8-ounce, or 225 g) salmon fillets

2 tablespoons (6 g) thinly sliced fresh garlic chives (see recipe note)

Soak a cedar plank in water for at least 1 hour before you plan to grill.

Prepare a medium-hot two-zone fire in a charcoal grill (see page 13) with a grill grate over the coals.

In a small bowl, stir together the honey, soy sauce, sesame oil, vinegar, ginger, and garlic. Reserve half the glaze and set aside until needed.

Place the salmon in a shallow dish and thoroughly pat dry with paper towels. Generously brush the fillets with the remaining glaze. Sprinkle an equal amount of chives over each fillet.

Preheat the plank until it starts to smoke (see page 194). Turn the plank over and move it over indirect heat. Arrange the salmon on the plank and drizzle the fillets with any glaze that dripped off into the dish. Close the grill lid. Grill for 15 to 20 minutes, until an instant-read thermometer inserted into the thickest part of the flesh reaches 120°F to 125°F (49°C to 52°C). (Depending on the thickness of your fillets, cooking time may vary by a few minutes.)

On the stovetop, in a small saucepan over medium heat, bring the reserved glaze to a simmer. Spoon the warm glaze over the salmon before serving, or offer it as a sauce for side dishes.

RECIPE NOTE
Garlic chives, a relative of the more common onion chives (or what we simply call "chives"), have flat, broad leaves and a delicate garlic flavor. They can be found in most Asian grocery stores and some specialty markets. Substitute regular chives or scallions as needed.

HOT TIP

To form a rectangular pizza that will fit your plank, shape the dough into a cylinder and roll it out on a smooth surface. Drape the dough over a clean spare plank. With your fingers, shape or roll up the edges as needed to fit perfectly on the plank. The dough can then be pricked all over with a fork, misted with cooking spray, and carefully flipped over on top of your preheated plank.

PEACH AND PROSCIUTTO PLANKED PIZZA

Using an aromatic wood plank is a worthwhile alternative to grilling on a pizza stone or directly on the grate. It infuses the crust with a light, smoky flavor, keeps the dough from burning underneath, and makes a great presentation on the table. I like to make this vibrant pizza—full of sweet, ripe peaches, fragrant basil, and wisps of salty prosciutto—when I'm looking to do something a little different from my usual veggie garden and pepperoni pie.

MAKES 4 SERVINGS

1 pound (454 g) Homemade Pizza Dough (page 163) or store-bought pizza dough

1 teaspoon olive oil

1 teaspoon balsamic vinegar

Kosher salt

Ground black pepper

1 to 1½ peaches, pitted, halved, and cut into ½-inch (1 cm) wedges

Olive oil cooking spray, for misting

Coarse-grind cornmeal, for dusting

2 cups (230 g) shredded mozzarella cheese

6 thin slices prosciutto, torn into pieces

¼ red onion, thinly sliced

½ cup (75 g) crumbled goat cheese

Handful thinly sliced fresh basil

Soak two maple or alder planks in water for at least 1 hour before you plan to grill.

Bring the chilled pizza dough to room temperature for at least 30 minutes.

Prepare a medium-hot two-zone fire in a charcoal grill (see page 13) with a grill grate over the coals.

In a small bowl, whisk the olive oil, vinegar, and a pinch each of salt and pepper until well blended. Add the peach wedges and toss to coat. Set aside until needed.

Divide the dough in half and shape each portion into a long smooth cylinder. Roll each cylinder into a rectangle about the size of your plank (see tip). Prick the dough all over with a fork and mist the surface with cooking spray.

Preheat the first plank until it starts to smoke (see page 194). Turn the plank over and move it over indirect heat. Dust the surface with a handful of cornmeal (to keep the dough from sticking). Place the first dough, oiled-side down, on the plank and mist the top with cooking spray. Close the grill lid. Grill for 5 to 7 minutes, until lightly browned and slightly crisp.

Working quickly, spread half the mozzarella on the crust (all the way to the edges), followed by half each of the prosciutto, onion, peaches, and goat cheese. Close the grill lid. Continue grilling for 5 to 7 minutes, until the cheese is golden and bubbly and the toppings are warmed through.

Garnish the pizza with basil before serving. Repeat the process with the second plank to make the second pizza.

CHAPTER 8

OUTDOOR SWEETS

Sticky spoons and forks drip with sweet sustenance. In just a few seconds, they're licked clean. Crumpled napkins sit on empty plates as the coals burn out, the sky turns a deeper black, and the stars glow brighter. Conversations quiet into comfortable silence. You feel your body aligning itself with the rhythm of the earth, and in that moment, life is complete.

CAMPFIRE S'MORES, 6 WAYS

A camping cookbook just isn't complete without s'mores! But you don't need a recipe to tell you how to toast a marshmallow. Rather, think of these "recipes" as inspiration for your next campfire concoction when you want to jazz up the usual marshmallow, chocolate, and graham cracker stack.

STRAWBERRY S'MORES

Toasted marshmallows

Strawberries (fresh or warmed over the fire)

Dark chocolate

Graham crackers

PEANUT BUTTER AND BANANA S'MORES

Toasted marshmallows

Sliced bananas

Reese's Peanut Butter Cups

Chocolate graham crackers

CHOCOLATE CHIP COOKIE S'MORES

Toasted marshmallows

Milk chocolate

Soft-baked chocolate chip cookies

NUTELLA AND SALTED CARAMEL S'MORES

Toasted marshmallows

Nutella

Salted caramel chocolate

Graham crackers

ALMOND BUTTER AND JELLY S'MORES

Toasted marshmallows

Raspberry jelly

Almond butter

Dark chocolate with almonds

Graham crackers

NUTTY CARAMEL S'MORES

Toasted marshmallows

Crunchy peanut butter

Caramel chocolate

Chocolate graham crackers

S'MORES TIPS & TRICKS

Everyone has an idea of the perfect s'more. Should the chocolate be melted or not? Should the marshmallow be well charred or just golden brown? While there's no right or wrong when it comes to making the classic treat, I've toasted (and burned) many a s'more in my life, so here are a few things I've learned along the way.

You don't have to toast a marshmallow on a stick.

In fact, you don't need skewers at all. Simply assemble your s'more in the center of a sheet of heavy-duty foil, wrap it up tightly, and place it on the grill grate or near the coals for a few minutes. Use tongs to retrieve your foil pack. The marshmallow won't have a golden crust, but it'll be perfectly gooey, along with the chocolate and other ingredients.

A toasted marshmallow doesn't actually melt the chocolate.

The residual heat from a hot-off-the-flame marshmallow *might* make the top of the chocolate glisten, but it certainly won't melt it into an oozing cascade. Instead, melt your ingredients separately. Place a square of chocolate on a graham cracker, and set it over indirect heat on the grill grate. Pull it off once the chocolate has melted sufficiently, and top with a toasted marshmallow.

It's easy to make s'mores for a crowd.

To melt several s'mores at the same time (or if you have quite the raging fire going), place a cast-iron pan on the grate and arrange your chocolate-laden graham crackers in the pan. Transfer them to plates with a spatula once melted. The pan method also helps prevent your crackers from scorching or falling through the grate. Campers will want to toast their own marshmallows, of course!

You don't need a campfire to make s'mores.

If you have a portable grill with a lid, you can make s'mores without making a fire. Stack a graham cracker, chocolate, and marshmallow on the grate, leave the whole thing under the lid for a few minutes, and the ingredients will melt beautifully.

You can let your imagination run wild.

If you've never ventured outside of graham cracker/milk chocolate/marshmallow territory, you are in for a treat.

Step up your s'more game with different kinds of crackers and cookies, like flavored graham crackers (cinnamon or chocolate), oatmeal cookies, vanilla wafers, gingersnaps, or stroopwafel. Even pound cake, brownies, Pop-Tarts, or Rice Krispies treats can serve as tasty bases!

Explore different types of chocolate, like white, dark, and extra dark chocolate, or artisanal flavors like salted caramel, chile orange, and mint chocolate.

Experiment with your favorite jams, jellies, or nut butters, as well as caramel sauce, chocolate syrup, or fresh berries.

SOME MORE HISTORY

The history of the s'more is somewhat vague, but the first recipe for "Some Mores" was published in 1927 in a handbook called Tramping and Trailing with the Girl Scouts. Though the recipe was credited to a woman named Loretta Scott Crew, sources are conflicted on whether she actually invented the sticky snack or was merely the first to be formally credited for it. The original recipe instructs Girl Scouts to "Toast two marshmallows over the coals to a crisp gooey state and then put them inside a graham cracker and chocolate bar sandwich. . . . Though it tastes like 'some more,' one is really enough." As for when "some more" became "s'more," the contracted term came a decade later in various publications and has stuck ever since.

COAL-BAKED BANANA BOATS

These melty, mouthwatering treats are a camping tradition for my crew. When the fire is starting to wane and we're yearning for a midnight snack, we put a few of these foil packs on the glowing hot embers. The bananas turn so creamy that it's almost like eating a chocolaty peanut butter and banana soufflé. They're also completely customizable and our banana boats differ slightly each time, depending on what we remember to buy or pack. To start your own tradition, create a "build your own" banana boat bar and let your friends concoct their own campfire dessert.

MAKES 4 SERVINGS

---

4 medium bananas

½ cup (135 g) peanut butter

½ cup (45 g) chocolate chips

½ cup (57 g) chopped pecans

Prepare a bed of glowing hot coals in a fire pit.

With the peels still on, split each banana in half, stopping just before you slice through to the bottom. Fill each banana "boat" with equal portions of the peanut butter, chocolate chips, and pecans. Wrap each banana boat tightly with aluminum foil and place the packets directly on top of the hot coals. Cook for about 10 minutes, until the bananas are soft and the chocolate chips are melted.

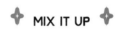 MIX IT UP

These banana boats are good with just about anything—try topping them with walnuts, marshmallows, almond butter, peanut butter chips, caramel sauce, or crushed graham crackers (you know, the ones sitting in the bottom of the box that nobody wants for a s'more).

MAKES 4 SERVINGS

2 tablespoons honey

2 teaspoons ground cinnamon

1 cup (227 g) crème fraîche

4 pears, halved and cored

RECIPE NOTE
I like to use Bartlett pears for this recipe, but any variety will work.

GRILLED PEARS WITH HONEY-CINNAMON CRÈME FRAÎCHE

These pears are light and silky and pair nicely with a glass of rosé or white wine, which is always a good way to end the day.

Prepare a grill over medium-high heat.

Meanwhile, stir the honey and cinnamon into the crème fraîche (right in the container for easy cleanup) until well combined.

Place the pears on the grill and cook for 3 to 5 minutes, turning once, until the pears are softened with good grill marks.

Serve each pear with a dollop of the sweetened crème fraîche.

MAKES 4 SERVINGS

2 tablespoons butter

2 tablespoons packed brown sugar

4 medium figs, halved lengthwise

2 medium peaches, pitted and sliced

SWEET CARAMELIZED FIGS AND PEACHES

If your sweet tooth is aching after dinner but you don't feel like making a production out of dessert, these caramelized figs and peaches will satisfy on both counts. Just a few minutes in a browned butter glaze brings out their richness without overpowering their fresh flavor. Serve them with a slice of pound cake, or spoon over yogurt for a lighter option.

In a small saucepan over medium heat, melt the butter. Add the sugar and stir until the mixture turns frothy and golden brown, about 2 minutes.

Add the figs and peaches and stir to coat. Cook until the fruits start to soften and release their juices, about 3 minutes, stirring occasionally.

Divide the fruit among serving plates, spooning the glaze over the fruits.

3 cups (360 g) Multipurpose Baking Mix (page 32)

2 cups (475 ml) buttermilk

Olive oil spray

1½ pounds (680 g) strawberries, hulled and halved

2 stalks rhubarb, sliced

½ cup (50 g) sugar

½ cup (113 g) butter, cut into small pieces

DUTCH OVEN STRAWBERRY-RHUBARB COBBLER

For years, I used to make the camp cobbler found in every Scout cookbook, the one with a box of cake mix and a few cans of fruit. Then I graduated to using fresh fruit . . . along with the cake mix, because by the time I decided I wanted to make cobbler in camp, we were already at the supermarket, and picking up a box was much easier than buying everything in it. There's a reason that Scout cobbler is so popular; it's super easy, super convenient, and four fewer things to think about on your shopping list. But if you make the baking mix ahead of time at home, you can have the same ease and convenience of a box—minus any questionable ingredients.

MAKES 6 TO 8 SERVINGS

Prepare a mound of wood coals, hardwood lump charcoal, or charcoal briquettes (see page 12).

Meanwhile, whisk together the baking mix and buttermilk in a large bowl until the batter is well blended.

Lightly spray a dutch oven with oil (or cover with a disposable liner, see "Quicken Your Cleanup," left) and add the strawberries and rhubarb. Stir in the sugar until combined. Pour the batter over the fruit and spread the pieces of butter evenly on top.

Move about a quart's worth of coals to the cooking pit and arrange them in a ring (see page 120). Set the oven on the ring of coals, cover, and place 1½ rings of coals on the lid.

Bake over medium heat for 20 to 25 minutes, until the crust is golden brown.

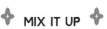 MIX IT UP

Use any combination of fruits in this recipe, or just use your favorite one. Generally, I aim for 1½ to 2 pounds (680 to 900 g) of fruit in a cobbler.

QUICKEN YOUR CLEANUP

No matter how much you love dutch oven cobblers, there's no denying they can be sticky, messy, and hard to clean—especially at night when the last thing you want to do is scrape and season your cast iron. To simplify cleanup, line the inside of the oven with a double layer of heavy-duty aluminum foil, allowing several inches of overlap to prevent the juices from seeping through the seam. You can also use disposable parchment liners or aluminum liners that are made specifically for dutch ovens. The aluminum ones resemble deep pie pans and are sized and shaped to fit inside a standard oven.

HIGH-ALTITUDE BAKING TIP

If you're making a dutch baby in camp at an elevation above 3,000 feet (900 m), a quick and dirty trick for helping the pancake puff up is to use extra-large eggs or high-protein flour in the batter, or both. The science behind this is to increase the protein sources so that coagulation can occur before the structure collapses (as a result of low air pressure). For campsites at 5,000 feet (1,500 m), try adding 1 large egg plus 1 to 2 tablespoons flour to the batter. For campsites at 8,000 feet (2,400 m) or above, try adding 2 large eggs plus 2 to 4 tablespoons flour to the batter.

Remember that elevation and humidity can vary greatly on every camping trip, so you may need to experiment with varying amounts of egg and flour before you find the perfect ratio. But no worries if your dutch baby doesn't pass the puff test—it will still be delicious.

APPLELICIOUS DUTCH BABY

A dutch baby is one of those dishes that can go from breakfast to dessert and back to breakfast again. It's basically an eggy pancake—or a marriage of a pancake and a popover, if you will. Though it's typically served for breakfast, a dutch baby makes a sweetly satisfying dessert when topped with lots of luscious fresh fruit and warm brown sugar. (At home, try it with a scoop of ice cream!) It's sometimes called a German pancake, from which it was derived, and the term Dutch refers to the German-speaking immigrants known as the Pennsylvania Dutch.

MAKES 6 SERVINGS

1 cup (120 g) all-purpose flour

½ cup (106 g) packed brown sugar, divided

½ teaspoon ground cinnamon, divided

6 large eggs

1 cup (240 ml) milk

Olive oil spray

¼ cup (56 g) butter

3 medium apples, cored and cut into ¼-inch (6-mm) slices

Powdered sugar

At Home: Combine the flour, ¼ cup (103 g) of the brown sugar, and ¼ teaspoon of the cinnamon in a resealable plastic bag and store in a dry, cool place until ready to use.

In Camp: Prepare a mound of wood coals, hardwood lump charcoal, or charcoal briquettes (see page 12).

Meanwhile, whisk together the eggs, milk, and flour mixture in a medium bowl until well blended.

Move about a quart's worth of coals to the cooking pit and arrange them in a ring (see page 120). Lightly spray a dutch oven with oil and heat it over the coals. Melt the butter in the oven, then pour in the egg mixture. Spread the apples evenly over the surface and sprinkle with the remaining ¼ cup (103 g) sugar and the remaining ¼ teaspoon cinnamon. Cover and place 1½ rings of coals on the lid.

Bake over medium heat for 20 to 25 minutes, or until the pancake is puffed and golden all over. (Call the kids over to ooh and ahh at your creation once you take the oven off the heat, because the pancake will deflate shortly after the lid is removed.)

Dust the pancake with powdered sugar before serving.

 MIX IT UP

Try this recipe with pears, or half apples and half pears. If it's summertime and you want to take advantage of seasonal berries (imagine how beautiful it would be if you could forage wild blackberries near camp?), bake the dutch baby with any combination of berries and scatter a handful of fresh berries on top before serving.

CHAPTER 9

OUTDOOR DRINKS

After a long day in your backyard, setting up your cabin, or trekking through the backcountry, you will be thirsty. These fun and easy to make cocktails will cool you off or warm you up depending on the time of year.

MIMOSA SANGRIA

Mimosa is why long, lazy mornings exist. Sangria is why long, lazy afternoons exist. Put them together and you might as well park yourself in that hammock for the rest of the day. What I like most about this recipe is that it's more of a loose guideline, open to endless variations, and hard to mess up. You can mix and match your favorite fruits, juices, and liqueurs to create a signature cocktail that's probably way too easy of a pour (or "highly drinkable," as they say in the booze world). Better make a double batch for brunch!

MAKES 8 TO 10 SERVINGS

3 cups (700 ml) fruit juice

3 cups (750 g) fresh fruits (sliced or diced, if necessary)

½ cup (120 ml) fruity liqueur (such as Cointreau, Grand Marnier, or Chambord)

1 (750 ml) bottle dry sparkling wine, chilled

Combine the juice, fruit, and liqueur in a large jar (or pitcher, if serving from one) and let the flavors intermingle for at least 1 hour. If you have space in your cooler, keep the mixture chilled until ready to use.

Add the sparkling wine to the jar (or pitcher) and serve immediately. Alternatively, you can fill individual glasses about one-third full with the juice mixture and top with sparkling wine.

RECIPE NOTE
In the recipe pictured, I used a blend of orange and pineapple juices, sliced strawberries and whole blueberries, Cointreau, and Prosecco.

3 parts limeade

2 parts silver tequila

1 part triple sec

Jalapeño pepper, thinly sliced (optional)

3-2-1 MARGARITA

A classic margarita is an incredibly simple beverage to concoct: just tequila, triple sec, and lime juice. But when you want to keep it even simpler in the backcountry, limeade is a clever cheat that almost makes it taste like the real thing. Ratios for margaritas can vary but here's an easy one to remember in camp: 3 parts limeade, 2 parts tequila, and 1 part triple sec.

Combine the limeade, tequila, and triple sec in a glass and top off with ice. If you like your margarita with some heat, stir in a few slices of jalapeño before serving.

1 part silver tequila

1 part grapefruit soda

Juice of ½ medium lime

Kosher salt

PALOMA

Margaritas (right) may be the most well known of Mexico's cocktails on this side of the border, but the Paloma (left) tops the list as a traditional favorite in the country. Fizzy, invigorating, and smooth, it's exactly what you want on a hot, lazy, leisurely day by the water. You can try any brand of grapefruit soda, such as Izze, Hansen's, Blue Sky, San Pellegrino, or even Squirt or Fresca, but Jarritos is the most popular mixer, if you can find it.

Combine the tequila, grapefruit soda, and lime juice in a glass. Add a pinch of salt, top off with ice, and serve.

1 part light lager or wheat beer, chilled

1 part ruby red grapefruit juice, chilled

MIX IT UP

Try a variety of fruit juices and nectars to craft your own signature shandy, such as orange juice, pomegranate juice, mango nectar, pear nectar, apple cider, lemonade, or the Hawaiian blend of POG (passion fruit, orange, guava).

RUBY RED GRAPEFRUIT SHANDY

English speakers know this drink as a shandy, but around the world it goes by a number of other monikers: panaché (France), clara (Spain), radler (Germany), and Sneeuwwitje ("Snow White" in Holland). Whatever you call it, there's no arguing that this refreshing beer cocktail is easy drinkin'. Though a few commercial breweries have packaged their own versions of shandies, it's a simple concoction to make in camp: just combine beer and juice. It's equally good for improving a beer you're not keen on, or enhancing a beer you already enjoy.

Pour the beer into a glass, then top with the juice. (Pictured left.)

Handful of fresh basil leaves

2 medium peaches, pitted and thinly sliced

2 (12-ounce/350 ml) bottles summer ale, chilled

1 cup (240 ml) ginger beer, chilled

1 cup (240 ml) peach nectar, chilled

MIX IT UP

If you're not traveling far, you can use sliced frozen peaches in place of fresh peaches to keep the sangria colder longer.

SUMMER ALE SANGRIA WITH GINGER AND PEACH

When you can't make up your mind between beer and sangria for happy hour, try a beer sangria—the happy-go-lucky, sun-kissed love child of two very respectable beverages. It's fresh, fruity, and fizzy, and makes the most of seasonal summer ales that show up for those few glorious months. Look for a light, bright, and crisp ale with notes of citrus or stone fruits to balance the spicy ginger beer and fresh ripe peaches.

In a stockpot, muddle the basil and half the peaches. Add the remaining peaches and the ale, ginger beer, and peach nectar and stir to combine. Serve immediately. (Pictured right.)

HONEY BOURBON LEMONADE

I like a good old-fashioned lemonade, but I love a good old-fashioned lemonade spiked with a shot of honey bour-bon (such as Wild Turkey American Honey or Jim Beam Honey). The sweetness of the bourbon goes down smooth and adds just the right amount of booze to the kind of beverage you want to slowly swill all day by the lake. (Hey, nothing wrong with that.)

MAKES 6 TO 8 SERVINGS

5 cups (12 dL) water, divided

1 cup (100 g) sugar

1 cup (240 ml) freshly squeezed lemon juice

1 cup (240 ml) honey bourbon

1 large lemon, thinly sliced

At Home: Combine 2 cups (475 ml) of the water and the sugar in a small saucepan over medium heat. Stir until the sugar is dissolved, then remove from the heat and let the simple syrup cool to room temperature.

Pour the syrup, lemon juice, bourbon, and remaining 3 cups (725 ml) water into a half-gallon container. Depending on the acidity of your lemons, adjust for taste and add more sugar, lemon juice, or water as needed. Chill for up to 1 week.

In Camp: Serve the honey bourbon lemonade over ice and garnish with lemon slices.

LEMONADE LOVE

A good lemonade starts with the above recipe of simple syrup, lemon juice, and water. Make it even better with one of the flavor variations below.

For Herbal Lemonade: Steep a few sprigs of thyme, rosemary, mint, or basil in the simple syrup over low heat for about 30 minutes. Discard the herbs and combine the infused syrup with lemon juice and water as directed above.

For Strawberry Lemonade: Add 1 cup strawberry puree to the lemonade. Or take it a step further and use a basil-infused syrup for Strawberry-Basil Lemonade.

For Pink Lemonade: Add 2 tablespoons grenadine to the lemonade.

For Spa Lemonade: Use a mint-infused syrup and steep sliced cucumbers in the lemonade for at least 2 hours (and no more than 2 days) before serving.

For Arnold Palmer: Replace the water with strong brewed green, black, or white tea.

For Limeade: Replace the lemon juice with freshly squeezed lime juice.

WHISKEY-SPIKED SWEET TEA

Iced tea cocktails like this one are a modern spin on mixed drinks that let both beverages shine. The whiskey here (I like to use Tennessee whiskey) adds just enough bite to counter the sweetness of the Southern-style tea. But be warned: It goes down way too easily.

MAKES 6 TO 8 SERVINGS

7 cups (17 dL) water

1 cup (100 g) sugar

3 family-size black iced tea bags

1 cup (240 g) whiskey

1 large lemon, thinly sliced

At Home: Bring the water to a boil in a large kettle. Remove the kettle from the heat and add the sugar and tea bags. Steep for about 5 minutes, stirring occasionally, until the sugar is dissolved.

Remove the tea bags, squeeze the liquid out, and discard. Let cool, then transfer the sweet tea to a half-gallon container. Stir in the whiskey and chill for up to 3 days.

In Camp: Serve the spiked sweet tea over ice and garnish with lemon slices.

RECIPE NOTE

Lipton and Luzianne are the standard supermarket brands formulated for iced tea brewing. These are not cold brew bags, but rather tea bags that still require hot water. They're labeled as "iced tea bags" because the tea won't turn cloudy when refrigerated. You can also use your favorite black tea in this recipe; simply replace the 3 family-size tea bags with 6 regular-size tea bags.

MAKE-YOUR-OWN CAMP COFFEE KIT

If you're serious about your cup of joe in the morning and instant coffee just isn't cutting it, consider making your own camp coffee kit. By storing all of your backcountry barista tools in one place, like a pouch or plastic bag, you can have a smoother and easier start to the day when your brain feels like a blur. Below are two of my favorite no-fuss brewing systems for camping.

For 1 or 2 people:

+ An **AeroPress Coffee and Espresso Maker**. The compact brewing system can make a mug of coffee in less than a minute, and it rinses clean in a snap. Simply add your coffee grinds, fill with hot water, and press the plunger for 20 seconds.

+ A small bag of your favorite **coffee beans**. If you're only making coffee for yourself and/or your partner, treat yourself to whole beans and make a fresh grind every morning.

+ A **hand coffee grinder** for grinding beans in camp. To save space, look for a coffee grinder that's specially designed to nest inside the AeroPress.

+ An **insulated mug**. Forget enamelware mugs, which are charming but impractical for coffee. Pack a double-wall insulated mug, preferably with a lid.

For 4 or more people:

+ A **GSI Outdoors Collapsible Java Drip**. This lightweight silicone drip coffeemaker fits over any wide-mouth bottle and makes pour-over style coffee—just add grinds and hot water. When done, it collapses into a disk for easy storage.

+ A **vacuum-insulated bottle or carafe** for keeping the coffee hot while your campmates trudge to the kitchen.

+ A pack of **#4 coffee filters**.

+ A bag of **freshly ground coffee beans**. Store them in a dry, cool place, preferably in an airtight container, to maintain freshness.

+ An **insulated mug** for each person.

CAMP CHAI

It may not be the most authentic chai, but the ease of having a jar of homemade chai concentrate on hand for spicy mugs of tea in camp cannot be beat. The sweetened condensed milk slips some comfort into warm tea that's most welcome on a chilly morning when you don't even want to get out of your sleeping bag, much less your tent. Mix it with a robust, strong-brewed black tea, such as Assam, English breakfast, or Earl Grey, for a classic chai. If you want to mix it up, try a lighter tea like Darjeeling.

MAKES UP TO 14 SERVINGS

FOR THE CHAI CONCENTRATE

1 (14-ounce/415-ml) can sweetened condensed milk

1 teaspoon ground cardamom

1 teaspoon ground ginger

½ teaspoon ground cinnamon

½ teaspoon ground cloves

FOR THE CHAI

Black tea bag

Hot water

At Home: To make the chai concentrate, combine all of the ingredients in a small bowl. Transfer to a lidded container and chill for up to 3 weeks.

In Camp: Steep the tea bag in a mug of hot water for 3 to 5 minutes. Stir in a few spoonfuls of chai concentrate to taste.

 MIX IT UP

Cardamom, ginger, cinnamon, and cloves are the core ingredients of any good chai, but you can customize the spice mix to your liking—try star anise, fennel, allspice, coriander, or even black pepper if you're feeling adventurous.

HOMEMADE HOT CHOCOLATE MIX

Those little packets of hot cocoa mix—you know, the ones with the dehydrated mini marshmallows in them—have a certain nostalgia that I sometimes can't resist. Chalk it up to years of camping and sipping mugfuls by a fire while trading stories about adventures and reminiscing on life. I think I like the memories associated with them more than I actually like the cocoa itself, though. So I set forth to make my own mix—one that includes real bits of chocolate and not just the dry powdery stuff. The combination of chocolate chips, cocoa powder, sugar, and a touch of dry milk powder (which you're free to omit if you always have milk on hand) makes a creamy, luscious mug of hot chocolate with deep flavor.

MAKES 14 TO 18 SERVINGS

1 cup (170 g) bittersweet chocolate chips, very finely chopped (at least 60% cacao)

1 cup (85 g) unsweetened cocoa powder

1 cup (100 g) sugar

½ cup (21 g) dry milk powder

½ teaspoon kosher salt

Combine all of the ingredients in a small bowl. Transfer to an airtight container and store in a dry, cool place for up to 3 months.

CLASSIC HOT CHOCOLATE

MAKES 1 SERVING

1 cup (240 ml) water or milk

3 to 4 tablespoons Homemade Hot Chocolate Mix (left)

Heat the water in a small saucepan over medium heat until steamy. Add the hot chocolate mix and stir until all of the ingredients are dissolved and well blended.

MEXICAN HOT CHOCOLATE

MAKES 1 SERVING

1 cup (240 ml) water or milk

3 to 4 tablespoons Homemade Hot Chocolate Mix (above)

⅛ teaspoon ground cinnamon

Pinch of ground cayenne pepper

Heat the water in a small saucepan over medium heat until steamy. Add the hot chocolate mix, cinnamon, and cayenne and stir until all of the ingredients are dissolved and well blended.

SNUGGLERS

This cocktail is near and dear to my heart because it's one that my friends and I have made hundreds of times on camping trips, cabin trips, and any mountain getaway where there's snow involved. More than a decade of Snuggler-fueled shenanigans have happened in at least six states and two countries! We only make this when we all get together on such a trip (which, sadly, is only once or twice a year these days with everybody scattered between both coasts), so it truly feels like a special occasion when someone breaks out the bottle of peppermint schnapps and little packets of cocoa. The cozy cocktail tastes like a warm, tingly, melty Peppermint Pattie in a cup. You can use any hot cocoa or hot chocolate in this recipe, but my Homemade Hot Chocolate Mix (opposite page) is especially heavenly with it.

MAKES 1 SERVING

1 part peppermint schnapps

6 parts Classic Hot Chocolate (opposite page)

Stir the schnapps into a mug of hot chocolate until well combined.

 MIX IT UP

Another variation I like to make is what I call Smugglers—a mix of Mexican Hot Chocolate (opposite page) and peppermint schnapps, sometimes with a splash of cognac.

CITRUS AND MAPLE MULLED WINE

Mulled wine is one of those things where everyone has a certain way of making it, and usually with a secret ingredient, kind of like barbecue sauce or the family pot roast. So, here's my secret ingredient: maple syrup. In the past, I'd always used sugar to sweeten the brew (because steeping brings out the sour tannic flavor in wine), but I found that maple syrup adds a deep, smooth sweetness that takes the mulled wine to another level. It pairs especially well with wines that have hints of dark fruit, like plum, currant, and blackberry. Go with a syrup on the darker side of the spectrum, such as Grade A: Dark Color Robust Flavor for its strong, almost brown sugar–like flavor.

MAKES 8 SERVINGS

2 (750 ml) bottles red wine

½ cup (120 ml) maple syrup

1 teaspoon coriander seeds

2 (3-inch/8-cm) cinnamon sticks

12 allspice berries

2 star anise

1 bay leaf

2 medium oranges, halved crosswise

½ cup (120 ml) brandy

Add the wine, maple syrup, and all of the spices to a stockpot over medium heat. Juice the oranges into the stockpot and add the rinds. Bring to a simmer, reduce the heat to low, and steep for at least 30 minutes to let the flavors develop. Stir in the brandy before serving and ladle into mugs, avoiding the orange rinds and spices.

WAKE UP THOSE SPICES

To bring out even deeper flavor in your spices, toast them in the stockpot over medium-high heat before adding the other ingredients.

VANILLA AND BOURBON MULLED CIDER

Warm and fragrant, this mulled cider sings with heady spices (and a hint of booze) without overwhelming the delicate apple aroma. It's more than just swirling in a few cinnamon sticks or tossing in a bag of generic "mulling spices." Having the right blend of spice helps balance and enhance the natural acidity and sweetness in the apples, and if you start with great cider, you'll end up with great mulled cider. Look for one that's deep in color and cloudy with good body.

MAKES 4 SERVINGS

1 quart (1 L) apple cider

2 (3-inch/8-cm) cinnamon sticks

4 cardamom pods, bruised with the side of a knife

4 cloves

¼ teaspoon coriander seeds

½ vanilla bean, split

½ cup (120 ml) bourbon

Add the cider and all of the spices to a small saucepan over medium heat. Bring to a simmer, reduce the heat to low, and steep for at least 30 minutes to let the flavors develop. Stir in the bourbon before serving and ladle into mugs, avoiding the spices.

RESOURCES

While most things you need for live-fire cooking can be found in your kitchen or local hardware or home improvement store, these are my favorite online resources for the gear seen and used throughout this book. Visit www.thebackyardfirecookbook.com for more of my go-to grilling gear.

GRILLS AND FIRE PITS

Kamado Joe:
kamado-style ceramic grills and hardwood lump charcoal
www.kamadojoe.com

Lowe's:
flagstone retaining wall blocks for DIY fire pits
www.lowes.com

Solo Stove:
portable fire pits
www.solostove.com

Weber:
charcoal kettle grills and chimney starters
www.weber.com

WOOD, CHARCOAL, AND FIRE STARTERS

Ace Hardware:
wood chips and wood chunks
www.acehardware.com

BetterWood Products:
fatwood
www.betterwoodproducts.com

Fogo Premium Hardwood Lump Charcoal:
hardwood lump charcoal
www.fogocharcoal.com

Super Cedar:
fire starters
www.supercedar.com

WoolyWood:
fire starters
www.amazon.com

COOKWARE, TOOLS, AND ACCESSORIES

Aerobie AeroPress:
coffee and espresso maker
www.aerobie.com/product/aeropress

Camp Chef:
folding grill grates
www.campchef.com

Grate Chef:
grill wipes
www.gratechef.com

Kai USA Pure Komachi 2:
ceramic knives
www.kaiusaltd.com

Lodge Cast Iron:
cast-iron Dutch ovens, skillets, and planchas
www.lodgemfg.com

Nalgene:
leak-proof bottles and jars
www.nalgene.com

New West Knifeworks:
American-made steel knives with leather sheaths
www.newwestknifeworks.com

ORCA Coolers:
roto-molded coolers
www.orcacoolers.com

Outset Grillware:
grilling utensils and accessories, wood planks, and wood chips
www.outsetinc.com

Serenity Health & Home Décor:
fire pit grates
www.serenityhealth.com

Stansport:
folding camp grills
www.stansport.com

ThermoWorks:
instant-read meat thermometers
www.thermoworks.com

PANTRY GOODS

Hmart:
gochujang, gochugaru, and kimchi
www.hmart.com

The Reluctant Trading Experiment:
Tellicherry peppercorns
www.reluctanttrading.com

Wan Ja Shan:
organic soy sauce and tamari
www.wanjashan.com

CAMPING EQUIPMENT AND SUPPLIES

Backcountry:
camping equipment and supplies
www.backcountry.com

Campsuds:
biodegradable multipurpose soap
www.sierradawn.com

Coleman:
camp stoves and general camping supplies
www.coleman.com

Dr. Bronner's:
biodegradable pure castile liquid soap
www.drbronner.com

GSI Outdoors:
outdoor cooking and camping gear
www.gsioutdoors.com

REI:
outdoor recreational equipment
www.rei.com

Thermos:
Stainless King™ vacuum insulated bottles
www.thermos.com

TravelChair:
camp chairs and tables
www.travelchair.com

ABOUT THE AUTHOR

After many miles traveled in pursuit of adventure, countless meals shared under the open sky, and a decade of growing her own food and raising backyard chickens, Linda Ly truly believes a life outdoors is a life well lived. Whether she's grilling, gardening, snowboarding, mountain biking, or exploring her new stomping grounds of the Pacific Northwest, there are few days where the snow or the rain keeps her inside. Linda writes about all these simple pleasures, as well as her evolving modern homestead, on her award-winning blog *Garden Betty*.

In the fall of 2017, Linda and her husband, Will Taylor, and their daughter, Gemma Lumen, moved to their dream town of beautiful Bend, Oregon. It was the best decision they ever made for their family.

Follow along on www.gardenbetty.com and www.thebackyardfirecookbook.com. And don't forget to check out the companion book, *The New Camp Cookbook*, if you agree everything just tastes better outside.

ABOUT THE PHOTOGRAPHER

While a love of photography budded at an early age, Will Taylor's true passion and image-making career all started one evening capturing the sun's setting rays across the stunning expanse of Lake Tahoe, high in the Sierra Nevada Mountains. With the click of the shutter, Will realized the inherent power of photography to freeze a moment in time and then project that place, that instance, to others, sharing the beauty and inspiration of that split second. That one photo launched Will into his new career, and now, decades later, he still captures the beauty of our natural world for clients ranging from Fortune 500 companies to the world's top fashion brands.

For Will's latest outdoor adventures in his new home in Central Oregon, where you'll find him mountain biking and snowboarding through the majestic beauty of the Cascade Mountains with his wife and daughter, visit www.instagram.com/willtaylorphotography.

INDEX